THE ETRUSCANS

LOST CIVILIZATIONS

The books in this series explore the rise and fall of the great civilizations and peoples of the ancient world. Each book considers not only their history but their art, culture and lasting legacy and asks why they remain important and relevant in our world today.

Already published:

The Aztecs Frances F. Berdan
The Barbarians Peter Bogucki
Egypt Christina Riggs
The Etruscans Lucy Shipley
The Goths David M. Gwynn
The Greeks Philip Matyszak
The Inca Kevin Lane
The Indus Andrew Robinson
The Maya Megan E. O'Neil
Nubia Sarah M. Schellinger
The Persians Geoffrey Parker and Brenda Parker
The Phoenicians Vadim S. Jigoulov
The Sumerians Paul Collins

THE ETRUSCANS

LOST CIVILIZATIONS

LUCY SHIPLEY

REAKTION BOOKS

For Silvia and Patrick

Published by Reaktion Books Ltd
Unit 32, Waterside
44–48 Wharf Road
London N1 7UX, UK

www.reaktionbooks.co.uk

First published 2017, reprinted 2019
First published in paperback 2023

Printed and bound in India by Replika Press Pvt. Ltd

A catalogue record for this book is available from the British Library

ISBN 978 1 78914 832 9

CONTENTS

CHRONOLOGY

7000 BCE	Neolithic migrants from the Near East spread throughout Europe, including Italy
3300	Ötzi 'the Iceman' dies and is preserved in the Italian Alps
1600–1200	Bronze Age Terramare and Apennine cultures flourish in Central Italy
1100–900	Proto-Villanovan cultures; development of biconical urn burial; hilltop fortified settlements
900–700	Villanovan period. Increased social stratification; increasing evidence for trade with both northern Europe and Greece and the Near East. Gradual adoption of inhumation burial
700	First Etruscan alphabet, the Marsiliana Tablet, made
675	Characteristically Etruscan black burnished bucchero pottery produced at Caere
675–50	Construction of first major structures (with tiled roofing systems) at Poggio Civitate

635	Adoption of black-figure vase painting technique in Athens after its invention in Corinth
625–550	Objects from the Isis tomb variously made and deposited
540	Destruction and abandonment of Poggio Civitate
535	Etruscan and Carthaginian ships defeat Greek forces in the Battle of Alalia off Corsica, following their expulsion from the island four years earlier
530	Development of Attic red-figure painting technique; subsequent adaptation in Etruria
509	Supposed date for expulsion of Etruscan kings from Rome
500	Gradual onset of economic recession in maritime centres of southern Etruria
484	Approximate birth of Herodotus
474	Defeat of Etruscan naval forces off Cumae marks the beginning of the end of Etruscan power in southern Italy, soon to be Magna Graecia
400	Migration southward of northern Celtic groups reduces Etruscan influence in northern Italy; they go on to sack Rome in 390

396	Siege of Veii, traditionally seen as the ending point for Etruscan political dominance
321	Theopompus of Chios dies in Alexandria
280	Defeat of Vulci by Rome
264	Defeat of Volsinii (Orvieto) after a popular revolt; Rome's attention turns to Carthage and the First Punic War begins
150–100	Piacenza Liver made and used
59 BCE–17 CE	Life of Livy, author of *History of Rome*
41–54 CE	Rule of Claudius, Roman emperor fascinated by already largely lost Etruscan culture
456	Bishop of Tarquinia referred to; Christianity has won
1296	First historical reports of Etruscan artefacts uncovered during defensive works at Arezzo
1435	Cosimo de' Medici comes to power in Florence
1513–21	Papacy of Leo X, son of Lorenzo 'il Magnifico' de Medici
1723	Thomas Dempster's *De Etruria Regali* republished by Thomas Coke
1726	Foundation of the Accademia Etrusca at Cortona

c. 1760–1820	'Etruscheria' or 'Etruscomania' sweeps Europe
1763	J. J. Winckelmann exposes 'Etruscan Vases' as Greek
1776	Foundation of the Museo Guarnacci at Volterra, the first public Etruscan museum
1796	Napoleon Bonaparte takes control of Italy; later his brother Lucien commences his archaeological investigations in Tuscany
1848	George Dennis presents his Etruscan adventures to an adoring public
1864	Garibaldi's March on Rome marks the beginnings of the modern Italian nation state
1867	The mummy wrapped in the Liber Linteus ends her travels in Zagreb
1922	Mussolini takes power in Italy; medieval city of Corneto renamed 'Tarquinia'
1927	D. H. Lawrence explores Tuscany; *Lady Chatterley's Lover* is published in Florence a year later
1939	Massimo Pallottino queries Herodotus; puts forward theory of indigenous Etruscan origins
1944	Division of Italy during last days of the Second World War; massacre at Marzabotto

1953	Discovery of DNA, later to become a major weapon in the fight over Etruscan origins
1964	Discovery of the Pyrgi Tablets
1985	First 'Anno degli Etruschi' celebration, repeated in 2015
2003	Discovery of the Tomb of the Infernal Chariot, Sarteano
2008	Financial crisis strikes; Italian banks with medieval pedigree begin to topple; funding for archaeology and heritage in Italy under threat
2016	First female ruler of Rome since Tullia, Virginia Raggi, elected

Prologue

Lost civilizations. The phrase conjures up visions of Indiana Jones barrelling across the desert and intrepid Victorian explorers fighting through thick jungle. These square-jawed heroes are searching for a city lost in the forest, or hidden beneath the sands – the archetype of a lost civilization. To be fair, there are places in the world where this heady mix of derring-do and archaeology come together. The iconic temples of Angkor, swathed in steamy rainforest; the first sight of Machu Picchu, high in the Andes. The nineteenth-century accounts of these discoveries are the stuff of legend. Yet it's a legend with major issues. In both these cases, Western explorers encountered a place that local people already knew all about. The very phrase 'lost civilization' is a denigration: modern descendants cannot possibly have any connection to those who once built these great monuments. The phrase implies that the living Khmer, or the indigenous people of the Andes, have nothing to do with their ancestors and can as such be treated poorly by colonists. A 'lost civilization' has to have become lost, actively forgotten by unworthy descendants. It can then be 'found' by archaeologists, exposed with their trowels, its treasures shipped off to museums, the lives of its people discussed in erudite journals. Yet the mystique remains, ensuring a separation between the living and the dead, keeping alive the dream of a better age, a knowledge that has been forgotten, a link that has been severed.

Etruscan musician from the Tomb of the Triclinium, Tarquinia.

At the other end of the scale of archaeological fantasy from a 'lost civilization' is the idea of a people who were 'just like us'. When textual sources survive and can be easily read, we can read the words of people long dead, busily occupied by their daily lives. Letters to friends or pleas for supplies, invitations to parties or admonitions to unruly children: these documents serve to underline the familiar. Texts, too, enable modern communities to claim shared values with ancient communities, to proudly proclaim allegiance to philosophies and concepts defined by thinkers and politicians who died thousands of years ago. The classic examples here are of ancient Greek and Roman culture, the acclaimed origin points for European political systems, legal rights, engineering ambition and much more. We do not talk about these civilizations as being lost, as they are still with us. The mixture of familiar activities and lofty ideals put forward in these texts results in recognition and acclamation: these people were just like us, they were just like who we want to be. Their darker elements are shuffled to one side: these are past people who we know, or we think we know.

These are two extreme kinds of reaction to the peoples of the past. Recognition and alienation; pull close and push away. Yet in between these extremes lie more complex and subtle emotional responses, to societies that are neither beguilingly familiar nor iconic survivors. They can be co-opted into the modern world, or conveniently mythologized and pushed to one side, dragged to one end of the scale or the other depending on what we want from them. Much of European prehistory falls into this strange abyss, with names from classical literature squished on to once-living groups, brought back to support this or that idea or a particular kind of nationalism. Myths cling to particular ancient communities, derived partly from mud flung in Athens or Rome, partly from Renaissance imaginations, partly from nineteenth-century rediscovery. This world before text can be remade in the image of the modern world, with evidence interpreted to suit the present day. These myths are tenacious, and can have the effect of pushing an ancient society to one end of the scale or the other, towards colonial ideologies of lost civilization or utopian visions of familiarity.

One of these prehistoric communities is the subject of this book. The lives of thousands of people, the places they lived in, the things they left behind: all have been stitched together into a myth of a lost civilization. They are not the oldest example of this trope: that honour can probably be awarded to the Minoans, as the most likely candidates for dwellers in 'Atlantis'. But the myth of the Etruscans began in antiquity, surged through the late medieval and Renaissance courts of Italy, fired revolution in the early nineteenth century, and skulked in the background of fascism. It is still going strong today, informing teenage romances and horror movies, while mayors and tourist offices struggle to sell tickets to sites and academics squabble over questions first posed two thousand years ago. Why does the Etruscan myth, the tale of a lost civilization within Europe, have such staying power? Where does it come from, and how does it intersect with the archaeological evidence we have? Most importantly of all, is this myth an appropriate story that is acceptable to keep telling?

For a people who challenged the dominance of Greece and threatened Roman ideas of superiority, the Etruscans remain well camouflaged behind the mythology these two cultures imposed upon them, and that we continue to engage with, when we bother to think about them at all. In the imagined world of the past, the glories of Rome cast a vast shadow over the Italian peninsula. Neighbours, rivals and eventually vanquished enemies of Rome, the relationship between the two cultures was ambivalent. Roman writers described Etruscan kings ruling over their city, but also their expulsion. Roman culture redeveloped Etruscan clothing and funeral games into cultural icons, yet Roman armies laid waste to the Etruscan heartlands of Tuscany as the city's reach expanded northwards. The siege of Veii in 396 BCE marked the beginning of the end for the Etruscans – yet Etruscan and Latin bilingual inscriptions continued to be read and written for centuries. Still, as Rome's sphere of influence grew, its Etruscan connections were largely forgotten – and this is certainly the case in terms of modern impressions of the Italian past. The intoxicating combination of familiarity and strangeness, the mix of bathroom humour and state-sponsored murder that is the signature of modern views of

Rome, leaves little space for older, more complicated inhabitants of the Italian peninsula. The Etruscans, if they do appear in the subconsciousness, are defined by half-remembered Victorian poetry (the enemies of brave Horatius, the captain of the gate[1]) and a dusty museum visited on holiday in Chiantishire. The aim of this book is to change that. I want to expose the Etruscans-as-lost-civilization myth, and introduce the archaeological evidence: the things that tell a deeper story. If you have picked up this volume, chances are you might be interested in the past, in the fortunes and possessions of peoples long dead. The purpose of this book is to inspire you to ask questions, to find out more: about the Etruscans themselves, and the making and manipulation of their legend.

ONE

Why do the Etruscans Matter?

One of the most striking objects to survive from the Etruscan period is hidden away in the great Louvre Museum in Paris. If you can wiggle your way around the *Winged Victory* and make your escape from the *Mona Lisa*, there lies a compelling piece of sculpted portraiture. It's an image of a man and a woman, with an intense intimacy in their pose. They lie propped up on their elbows, her body tucked into the curvature of his, their long legs close together, his bare feet nestling close to hers, encased in pointed boots. They are close to life-size, so when you approach you are gazing into two pairs of distinctively almond-shaped eyes. Below the eyes, on each clay face, is a faint smile – their mouths are slightly open, turned up at the corners, with a hint of amusement etched into their matching expressions. Both are gesturing with their hands – the woman's poised, almost in the act of telling a story. The man rests one arm upon her shoulder, leaning on his other elbow – his face is very slightly turned towards his companion. Their clothing is lovingly represented, its rich folds falling onto the bench on which they lie – the sumptuous pillows which cushion the embrace are not forgotten in this image of wealth, confidence and companionship. The perfect couple, fit to grace the pages of any modern gossip magazine.

There is a second incarnation of this sculpture in one of Rome's most wonderful and least visited museums too, the National Etruscan Museum housed in the gloriously crumbling palazzo of the Villa Giulia. The two sculptures come from the same place – a small town to the north of Rome, now almost entirely forgotten, in spite of its UNESCO listing. Cerveteri, ancient Caere, was one of the greatest cities of pre-Roman Italy. The man and woman displayed in the Louvre, and their counterparts in Rome, were part of the city's high society, a community so thoroughly erased that its only traces come from the tomb. For these sculptures are not solely aesthetically pleasing, designed to grace a home or temple like many of the other jewels of the Louvre's collection. They had a job to do, a purpose to serve: they are sarcophagi for the dead.

Who were these people? What was their real relationship like? Is their loving pose a piece of theatre for the grave, when in reality they nagged and bickered their way through a marriage gone sour? How did their family grow rich enough to bury them in this way, and why did they choose to spend their hard-earned resources on those who logically could not appreciate them? How did the couple die? Did they have children? Gazing into these faces sparks a hundred questions that the terracotta mouths will never be able to answer. Every archaeological find, from the humblest scrap of a roof tile to flashy gold jewellery, has this effect. It sets off a chain of queries that boil down to an essential concern, and a central comparison: how did these people live? And how do they affect our lives now? Only a few centuries after the Etruscans vanished as a distinct culture, people were asking these questions. We have continued to create answers ever since, creating a wilderness of ideas of what it was to be Etruscan. To try and ask again who this couple were, how they lived and how their lives impact upon our own is to navigate these intellectual badlands. Why begin on such an undertaking? Because the remnants and residues of Etruscan life and death, and the issues they force us to confront, are deeply relevant to the modern world – the hard questions and complex answers that make up Etruscan archaeology speak to some of the darkest, most difficult problems in our own lives.

The *Sarcophagus of the Spouses* (*c.* 520 BCE) is one of the most well-known icons of the Etruscan world, and it makes an ideal starting place for a journey through the central issues that define how we think about its occupants. One burial, however intriguing, is not enough to make a book. Each of the chapters that follow is focused on a different artefact or site: a place or a thing that poses a key question about the Etruscan people who made or inhabited it. There is a vast and growing corpus of Etruscan artefacts: I cannot bring it all to you without resorting to pages and pages of descriptions of pots, or interminable learned discussions on metalworking techniques. Instead, by focusing on a single object or single site, I want to focus your attention on a particular example. There are other sarcophagi, later than the examples in the Louvre or the Villa Giulia. I could describe them all and still we would be no closer to the central question of who this pair were, and what their lives were like. Big questions can be wrapped up in single objects and unique places, and it is those big questions that this book is about.

Why focus on the archaeology? Because it is the very materiality, the physicality, the toughness and durability of *things* and the way they insidiously slip and slide into every corner of our

Terracotta *Sarcophagus of the Spouses* from Cerveteri, discovered in 19th-century excavations and now in the Louvre, Paris.

lives that makes them so compelling. We tell ourselves that we are living in an increasingly digital world – but words and pictures are still created, stories still told through things. It is still to objects that we turn to present ourselves to the world; it's still the things we have that help define us. We are continually making and remaking ourselves, with the help of things. I would argue that the past is no different in this respect. It's through things that we can get at the people who made, used and ultimately discarded them – their projects of self-production are as wrapped up in stuff as our own. And always, wrapped up in these things, are fundamental questions about how we choose to be in the world, questions that structure our actions and reactions, questions that change and challenge how we think and what we feel. Questions and objects – the two mainstays of human experience.

Each object speaks to a key question, one that is still fiercely relevant. Filling in the centuries between the Etruscan object and the present day issue is a trail of texts. These writings are the work of people interested in the Etruscans, but trapped in their own ages and their own lives. Their experiences of the world in which they lived coloured their opinion of the objects they encountered, and resulted in the stories they told. This is easy to see in some cases – it is fairly straightforward to suppose that a medieval monk would have a particular agenda when writing about the Etruscans. Explicit political allegiances are often noticeable too – there is nothing subtle about Renaissance propaganda or Greek slander. There are, however, more subtle forms of manipulation of Etruscan things and Etruscan stories. Archaeological interpretations fall at this end of the scale. They are as fallible, as subjective, as a written source, in that they are produced by people, and people are the products of their experience. Even when pure science enters the picture, whether it is genetics or pollen sampling, it is still interpreted by a person. A person with an unavoidable, internalized agenda. As a result, this book is as much about the people who have written these stories as it is about the Etruscans themselves.

This book is organized in loose chronological order, which needs a little introduction. Splitting up time into chunks is an archaeologist's guilty pleasure, neatly separating the past into manageable sections that make thinking about huge spaces of time simple. Sometimes these splits are defined by specific events, but more usually, however, when archaeologists talk about different periods, they mean gradual changes in the style of objects. These are then assumed to mean shifts in lifestyle for their owners and makers. However, these changes in objects do not take place overnight. Instead they are stuttering transitions that cannot be pinned down to convenient decades and centuries, let alone tracked to a transformative moment at a set time one rainy Tuesday afternoon. This type of change overwrites historical events, particularly during prehistory when there is a distinct lack of these to go on. Cultural shifts and changes get stretched and manipulated to define amounts of time that don't make sense in terms of human lives. These are often then given names that speak more to the preconceptions of those doing the naming than what is actually happening in the archaeological record.

For example, in traditional terminology for Etruscan archaeology, the chunk of time from around 780 to 620 BCE is known as the Orientalizing period in central Italy, due to the popularity of a style seen as having been influenced by contact with the Near East. So a period of time, 160 years – between four and five lifetimes – is squashed into a single category. Think of everything that happens over one lifetime. Or even over a decade. While the speed of change might seem accelerated by increases in technological knowledge and its impact on our lives in the modern world, it is problematic to blur this amount of time and potential for change in human experience into one lump. Then, that lump is named after a group of artefacts, and every moment of that 160 years is characterized by a relationship with an external community. In a modern parallel, how appropriate would it be to term the period from 1900 to 2050 in Britain the 'Americanizing' period based on the adoption of American-influenced cultural practices? This naming protocol (laid out in Table 1) is largely borrowed from the periodization used to define the changes and developments in Greece, with adaptations for the Etruscan context.

PERIOD	DATES
Villanovan	950–780 BCE
Orientalizing	780–620 BCE
Archaic	620–450 BCE
Classical	450–300 BCE

Table 1: traditional periodization of Etruscan archaeology

The majority of the dates that feature in this book are those arrived at through more detailed stylistic studies. That is, they come from looking at changes in objects and using these to date archaeological features based on the sequence of design. By putting together the stylistic signatures of individual artefacts, and the combinations of things present, it is possible to provide a *terminus post quem* for the majority of archaeological contexts. This method is the bread and butter of archaeological dating. Of course, more absolute dating methods exist, with the best known being radiocarbon dating. This technique, which revolutionized archaeological dating in the mid-twentieth century, is based on the fact that carbon-14, a radioactive form of carbon absorbed by all living things, decays at a set rate. By analysing the amount of carbon-14 still present in the remains of any being that was once alive (a piece of animal bone or a burnt fragment of wood, for example), it is possible to arrive at the date at which the tree, animal or person in question died.

Unfortunately, radiocarbon dates for the Etruscan period are affected by what's known as the Hallstatt plateau, a problem named after the communities in Austria and Germany who were living at around the same time as Etruscan people. It's also known as 'the first millennium BCE dating disaster'. The issue arises from the need to match radiocarbon dates with calendar years. This is performed by comparing radiocarbon results with other forms of secure dating, such as the use of tree-ring data. Trees grow at different rates depending on each year's climate, creating distinctive patterns which can be matched up with passages of time. The calibration charts that connect these two series of data have an inconvenient flat point in the middle of the Etruscan period, with the result that dates from between 800 and 400 BCE can only be dated to this vast spread of time. Knowing this, the majority of archaeologists working on Etruscan material decide not to spend precious research funds on radiocarbon dates that provide a 'tell me something I don't know' answer.

Our glamourous couple, relaxing in the Louvre, can be dated by the style of their terracotta perch. They almost certainly date from the late sixth century BCE, around 525–500, a date which falls in the middle of the Archaic period. It reflects a moment in which the craftspeople of their city, Cerveteri, mastered the art of sculpture in clay. In addition to the two sarcophagi, the city's artisans produced intricate plaques and exquisite pots, which graced homes and, later, tombs. Frustratingly, the latter survive in far greater numbers and in better condition than the former. Indeed, at Cerveteri the houses of the dead are laid out according to a strict plan, and may echo the homes of the living: the sarcophagus lay at the heart of a city within a city, a place for the ancestors but reflecting the present.[1] The archaeological excavations at Cerveteri that exposed the sarcophagus seem equally frustrating to the modern reader, used to top technology, or at least diligent recording. While the Paris example was bought by Napoleon III in 1861, it was excavated sixteen years previously by the Marquis of Campana, an aristocrat obsessed by art and antiquities. At his home, the Villa Campana, the Marquis recreated an Etruscan tomb alongside real ancient monuments, including a chunk of Roman aqueduct.[2] Whether the tomb from which the reclining couple was removed had already been robbed is unclear: what is certain is that their bodies do not survive. We do not even know whether they had been cremated or buried entire beneath their terracotta effigies. It is difficult to even identify the tomb from which they came.

The world that our couple inhabited while living and breathing is even more difficult to get at. At least, with the help of some more recently acquired archaeological information, we can get a good idea of the surroundings of Cerveteri, and the environment in which Etruscan culture flourished. An hour's drive to the north of this Etruscan city lies the caldera of an extinct volcano, now filled by Lake Vico. The volcano stopped erupting around 138,000 years ago, leaving plenty of time for sediments to build up on the lake's bottom. Analysis of cores bored into this mud revealed ancient pollen particles trapped in the layers of dirt. Tracing these back through time, it has been possible for scientists to pinpoint the Etruscan period, and record the kinds of plants growing in the region at this time. The diversity is startling: over 750 different species are represented in pollen from this period, all associated with oak woodland.[3] Similar analyses of pollen from an Etruscan farmstead near the coastal town of Grosseto have solidified this image of this late Iron Age landscape: a heavily forested space with pockets of cleared land.[4]

This solid science rudely interrupts any reveries over the timelessness of the Italian landscape. The lands of the Etruscans, known collectively as Etruria, stretch upward from Cerveteri to incorporate the northern part of the province of Lazio, much of Tuscany and Umbria, and the southern piece of Emilia-Romagna. At the height of their power, Etruscan influence could be seen on the shores of the Adriatic just to the south of the Venetian Lagoon, and on the Bay of Naples. But it is this central area, roughly defined as between the Rivers Tiber and Arno, that is the Etruscan heartland. It encompasses some of the most attractive landscapes in Italy: lines of cypress trees next to golden rolling hills, scenes that inspired poets and artists and have ended up on calendars and screen savers. Even here, however, pockets of the ancient oak forest remain, known colloquially as *bosco*, or bush. There is still something primeval about these surviving forests that grow thicker as the Apennine Mountains begin. When the tourists have gone, snow falls here, a reminder that the Etruscans did not inhabit an eternal summer filled with wine and sunshine.

When the sun does shine, however, the heat is at its most intense on the western fringes of Etruria, the coastal region of the Maremma marshes. Grazed by cattle whose genetics feature heavily in the following chapter, this was once a dangerous malarial swamp. The introduction of drainage put paid to the mosquitoes, but the summer humidity and heaviness remains. The marshes are broken by slight rises and the occasional hilltop, the ascent of which still provides great relief from the sticky air below. Estuaries

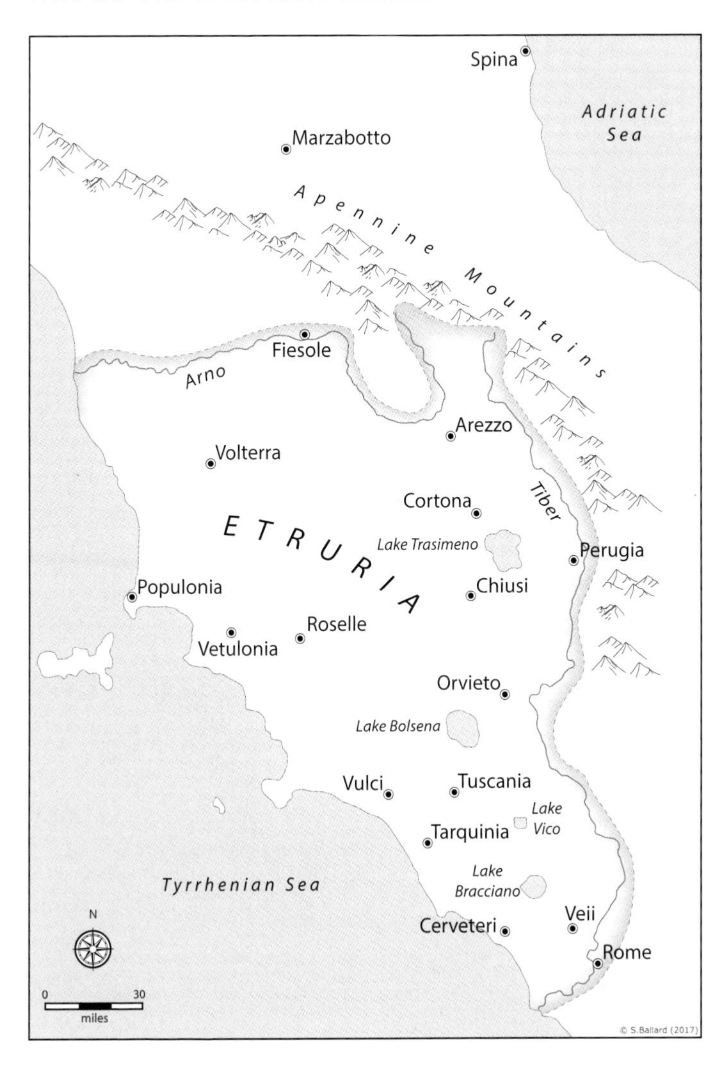

Map of Etruria and Latium.

drain into the Tyrrhenian Sea, a part of the Mediterranean with the Greek name for the Etruscans: Tyrhennoi. Further along the coast the marshland ends with the return of hills to the south, and inland lie a series of crater lakes: the aforementioned Lake Vico, but also Lakes Bracciano and Bolsena. Just beyond the shores of Lake Bracciano, the southernmost of this chain, the sprawl of Rome begins, and industrial towns struggle along on the flatlands of the Tiber Valley, with apartment blocks sprouting as the railway line becomes suburban, chugging inevitably to Roma Termini through cheerful graffiti-sprayed underpasses.

The medieval history of this region of Italy is largely responsible for its modern-day appearance. The city of Siena is a particularly good example: it has never recovered from the fourteenth-century Black Death, which reduced the city's population by almost two-thirds. Populations weakened by disease and famine were further threatened by roaming bands of mercenaries, including a ferocious group of English fighters who spilled southwards at the end of the Hundred Years War in France. The countryside emptied, with survivors banding together in hilltop settlements that were easily defended. Many of these hill towns have ancient origins, but the empty fields that lie between them would not have been familiar to Etruscan and Roman inhabitants of this landscape. The remains of Etruscan farmsteads have been found spread out across the region: small farms, where people made a living from fields cleared of the indigenous forest.[5] The great deforestation of the region began in the Roman period and was completed by the early Middle Ages, with far-reaching consequences. The loss of forest resulted in so much soil being eroded into the great rivers of Etruria that the coastline itself changed shape, a phenomenon most visible in the Tiber delta. The great Roman port of Ostia now lies 3 km inland, its trade a victim of the destruction that created the supposedly timeless Tuscan landscape.[6]

This was the world that our couple inhabited: a place of forests and clearings. The land may have made them rich enough to afford their elaborate burial; once the trees were cleared the soils of Etruria were famously fertile. Agricultural surplus exchanged for precious metals could be one way to get rich, but the soils of Etruria held another potential source of income. This is one of the richest sources of metal in the Mediterranean. Copper ores were perhaps the most lucrative of the metals to be removed from the Tuscan hills, used in the production of bronze, but silver and lead were also being extracted. Iron ores were another important source of wealth, with reserves particularly concentrated on Elba, with evidence for smelting found in the coastal city of Populonia. The expertise of Etruscan craftspeople was gained from direct exposure to high-quality metals produced on their doorstep. Both the items they made, and the refined ingots ready for working, could have been traded and stored, exchanged and saved – a further natural source of riches.

The Louvre sarcophagus is the product of the lands of Etruria at a specific moment in their history. It is also, however, part of a network that extends far beyond Italy. The bright colours with which it was decorated have parallels to the East, in what is now Turkey. Their smiling faces, too, may have been influenced by the fashionable Ionic style. The perfume which the woman is represented as holding would have come from further afield. It could have been scented with costly oils and resins used both to anoint the dead and sweeten the bodies of the living, transported from the deserts of Arabia. The flow of people across and around the waters of the Mediterranean is exemplified in this sepulchre for two individuals who were part of an international community, sharing interests and fashions over vast distances. Ships criss-crossed the Mediterranean and overland trade crossed the Alps, with Etruscan-made artefacts turning up as far north as Germany. The Etruscans, even our seemingly peaceful couple, can only be understood as part of this complex world, as rivals and participants in an Iron Age melange, in which people and objects were continually moving. The issue of movement lies at the heart of the next chapter, which reaches back in time to explore the origins of the Etruscans. Origins are the building blocks of identity for many people, ancient and modern, and the underlying question of this chapter asks how and what we know about where the Etruscans came from, and why this idea of belonging is still so compelling in the twenty-first century.

The known and the unknown, the transient and the seemingly permanent, the lost civilization and the found one: these are the contrasts at the centre of this book. To investigate the Etruscans is to tease out the middle ground between these extremes, to examine the contrasting stories and tales that push our perception of these people from one side to another. However, the role that these issues played in the lives of the Etruscans was at least as strong as their hold over modern society. The rest of this book is dedicated to drawing lines between the two.

TWO

Where is Home?

Climbing up from the dark blue of the Tyrrhenian to the town of Tarquinia, hairpin bends lead you through housing and industrial units, linking the old medieval town to the modern beach resort below. Once you arrive at the top, you are confronted by Etruscan things – postcards, replicas, stickers on buses and posters in ice cream shops. If there is such a thing as an Etruscan tourist hotspot, it's here. The painted tombs, strung along the hillside on the opposite side of town, are the focus. Yet, as any archaeologist will tell you, it's always better to visit the museum first. The object at the core of this chapter can be found in the chambers of the Museo Archeologico Nazionale Tarquiniense, nestled in a medieval palazzo that provides a welcome relief from the summer heat. It dates to the late ninth or early eighth century BCE, making it the oldest artefact included in this book. It is made of a grey-black clay with a soft sheen to its surface, a fabric known as impasto that would later evolve into the material of one of the most beautiful art forms of the Etruscan world. This is a cinerary urn, used to contain the cremated ashes of a human being, or beings.

The earliest known examples of cremation in Italy are far to the south of Tarquinia, in Abruzzo and Puglia. Dating to the Neolithic, they are highly unusual.[1] Both contained the remains of children. The Abruzzo urn included the ashes of a woman, scattered over the remains of two children.[2] One of the children from Puglia shows evidence of trauma, raising questions about the purpose of their death and the need for such an unusual form of burial.[3] There

House urn from the Monterozzi necropolis, Tarquinia.

is a truism in archaeology that the dead do not bury themselves, and it is important to think pragmatically about what this means. The cremation of a body requires the investment of a large amount of time and effort to dispose of the dead. The burnt remains from Early Bronze Age cremations from Sa Figu, Sardinia, show that the bodies were exposed to temperatures of between 400 and 800°C.[4] The amount of material required to heat a pyre to that level is significant, even in a landscape that was more heavily forested than it is today. Once the fuel was gathered, the spectacle of burning would have been seriously impressive for those watching, a statement about the value of the deceased and a way of imprinting their memory on to those left behind.

By the Middle Bronze Age, this highly expensive form of burial was popular across Europe, where the so-called Urnfield societies of central Europe buried their dead in vast cremation cemeteries. One of the largest examples in southern Germany contained over ten thousand costly cremations. This method of cremating the dead arrived in the Italian peninsula at least a century after it became popular in northern Europe, and burial of the whole body continued alongside the newfangled urn burials. Other items seem to have spread southwards too, including styles of pottery and fancy designs in metalwork. Yet settlements remain unchanged, as far as we can tell from the archaeological record. People's lives were largely unaffected, although the manner of their burial was now no longer a default. For some, the implication is that with cremation and new styles of pottery came people, in spite of the unchanged villages and uncomfortable time gaps. So, from the very beginning, the Tarquinia urn is tied to a central and still compelling question: where did the Etruscans come from?

The Tarquinia urn embodies this idea perfectly – it's in the shape of a house. Objects like this one are usually termed 'hut-urns'.[5] Yet it only takes a glance to tell you that these buildings are more than the term 'hut' implies. This structure is impressive in stature, with decorative architecture cleverly worked into the design. The most striking indication of this is a series of roof beams poking out, forming a spine along the ridge of the building. They are crowned with the heads of birds, with beaks that look suspiciously like ducks. Each pair of heads faces outwards, away from each other and towards the viewer. The building is a circular shape, with a

Reconstructed biconical urn burial from the Museo Etrusco Guarnacci, Volterra.

square doorway marking the entrance. It was through this doorway that the charred and broken bone of the urn's occupant was placed. Other urns still retain a door, hung from holes just above the entry space. The outer surface is smooth and shiny, although the door is outlined with three lines. A ridge around the bottom bulges outwards. Inside, the remains are visible, little grey and white scraps of humanity broken into a thousand pieces.

It seems likely that urns like this one are representative of real-life houses.[6] That is, they depict a tradition of building design that reaches back to at least the Bronze Age. Such structures, built out of perishable wood and thatch, covered with daub (a mix of mud, straw, animal dung, hair and whatever else seemed like a good idea to the builders), do not survive as well as their stone-built successors. Archaeologically, it is often only the shadowy holes of the structural posts of the building that remain. In sites across central Italy, excavators have picked up on these delicate clues, allowing for the reconstruction of buildings from the turn of the first millennium BCE. These are very different from the Urnfield settlements to the north, where people lived in long rectangular dwellings.[7] Instead, they are similar to this urn – square proportioned, with rounded corners and a curving front aspect. The site of Gran Carro, now submerged beneath the waters of Lake Bolsena, was occupied from the thirteenth to the eighth centuries BCE, before being abandoned in around 750.[8] The waters of the lake preserved some of the perishable organic substances, revealing a village of houses built in a similar style to our urn – a village that survived both fire and flood to be rebuilt time and again on similar lines.

To return to the local context of our urn, by the time of its burial, Tarquinia was already a distinct settlement. People had come from smaller villages to live together in a larger community. They made their homes on the hill now known as the Civita, where excavations have exposed the remains of both this early settlement and the later Etruscan city – built over exactly the same site. It lies on a spur of hillside opposite the area where the urn was found, facing the site of the later medieval town. Surface finds across the plateau, predominantly broken pottery, in addition to sub-surface structures, suggest a small township that changed shape as structures were constructed, used, abandoned and reinhabited. However, away from the Civita site are the remains of a number of buildings near one of the major burial areas, the Arcatelle necropolis, which were aligned on an east–west axis. Someone, or several people, had a clear idea of how these structures needed to be placed within the wider settlement. This was an organized space, with houses, storage areas and what seems to be a ritual complex linked together by trackways that survive in the modern agricultural landscape.

The latter building is something of an enigma. Deep beneath the later temple complex, excavators found a pit containing the remains of a child. Dated to the late ninth century BCE, this burial was contemporary with the early phases of settlement on the plateau, and seemed to be marking out this area as different from the earliest development of Tarquinia as a city.[9] Confirming this idea is the fact that this was no ordinary child – tests on the remains have suggested that the child may have suffered from epilepsy, with the seizures that typify the disease perhaps taken as moments of communion with the world of the divine, or as prophetic visions. Later Etruscan myths tell of a child found in the earth by a ploughman near Tarquinia, who taught the people how to predict the future – of which more later. While it is tempting to draw lines between the legend and the archaeology, the key point made by this burial is that there was a continuity of belief, centred on a central important place; one that survived hundreds of years of change.

This continuity is important to consider if we return to the question at hand: who were the Etruscans? The people living at Tarquinia, who made the urn, built their homes and buried an unusual child in a special place? From the specific evidence discussed so far, and the archaeological evidence in general – styles of pottery and metalwork, continuous occupation of other sites like that of Gran Carro spread across the region – you would certainly think so. Yet the writings of ancient authors present a different story. Herodotus (*c.* 485–426), whose stories of origins have given him the status of the first devoted historian, describes the Etruscans as travelling to Italy from the Eastern Mediterranean – from Lydia, or modern Turkey.[10] He tells of a population crisis

Spectacular bronze Villanovan helmet from a 9th-century burial.

– too many people, not enough food. The solution was obvious to the king of Lydia, Atys, who made his people draw lots to determine their fate. His own son, one Tyrrhenus, was to lead the unlucky losers to a new land across the sea to which he gave his name. Landing in Italy, they quickly overcame the locals and established a new and prosperous kingdom.

It's a good yarn, with plenty of enjoyable ingredients – a handsome hero, a dangerous journey, a dysfunctional royal family. Yet by the Roman period, other historians were adamant that Herodotus was wrong. Livy, writing in the first century BCE, decreed that they were more closely related to northern European peoples – an idea that might tie up to the old conception of people moving in along with cremation burial during the Bronze Age, but which also neatly connects the Etruscans with then-current Barbarian foes.[11] Living and working in Rome, it could be argued that Livy, otherwise known as Titus Livius Patavinus, was probably in contact with families of Etruscan origin. These survivors, who had adapted to life under the rule of their southern neighbours and successfully integrated into the city's high society, could have shared their own oral histories and origin myths, if not written texts. The later Roman author Pliny the Elder (23–79 CE) agreed with Livy, linking the Etruscans to a people he called the Raeti, driven southwards by marauding Gauls.[12] Dionysius of Halicarnassus, a Greek scholar living in a by then Roman world, declared that the Etruscans were Italian, and always had been, discarding the fashionable idea of migration in favour of a more prosaic grass-roots narrative. Just to confuse things, Tacitus, a historian better known for his intimate portrait of Roman Britain, supported Herodotus' version of the story.[13] Like Livy, having lived and studied in Rome, Tacitus would also have had the opportunity to meet and speak with Etruscan descendants. If he heard their story from their own lips, Tacitus' informants obviously had very different views to those of Livy.

By the end of the Roman period, and with the destruction of Etruscan texts in the razing of Italy that followed the rise of Christianity and fall of Rome, the tale was tangled. Different stories supporting very different ideas of who the Etruscans really were emerged from the mess. Of course, none of these authors were Etruscan themselves. They were Greek or Roman, members of societies for whom the Etruscans were a menace, an enemy, a people apart. So each scholar whose interpretation of the origin myth is listed above links up their Etruscans with other threats of the time in which they were writing. Herodotus, writing in the fifth century BCE, looked east. His version connected the Etruscans (by then limiting Greek dominion in the Western Mediterranean) with the Lydians, a people incorporated into the Persian Empire. That is, the empire with whom the Greeks had been at war for the first 35 years of Herodotus' life. It was potentially an entirely natural act to link the enemies of Greece from the East with the threat in the West.

Centuries later, Livy was living and writing at a time when Roman dominance was swelling, as the late Republican and early Imperial conquests pushed northwards through Gaul, and at the very end of his life cementing control of the rebellious Alpine peoples of what is now Switzerland and Austria. Pliny and Livy's Etruscans were kin to these present-day foes, who would be vanquished in their turn and brought under Roman influence, just as their ancestral cousins had been. Dionysius of Halicarnassus, a Turkish-Greek who also supported this thesis, may have been delicately and deliberately removing the Etruscans from Lydia and equating them firmly with the homeland of Roman overlords.[14]

Eighth-century bronze situla showing geometric decoration also seen on biconical urns.

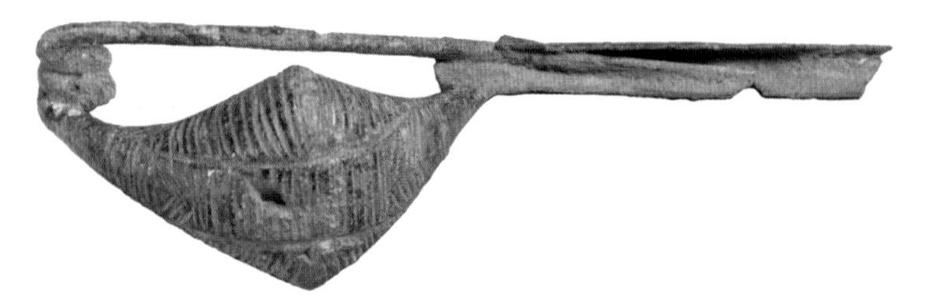

Simple Villanovan bronze fibula.

For Tacitus, the connection is less clear-cut – yet his preference for the Eastern model could conceivably be linked to his writings on another Eastern rebellion – the Jewish Revolt.[15] The Etruscans were recast once again as Eastern enemies of the state.

There is some archaeological evidence that could be construed as supporting the Eastern model of Etruscan origins. At the end of the eighth century BCE, between fifty and a hundred years after our urn was buried, a variety of objects influenced by design and fashion from the Eastern end of the Mediterranean begin to appear in Etruscan burials.[16] They show images that can be clearly linked to ideas from as far away as Iran, while raw materials from Egypt and sub-Saharan Africa pop up in Etruscan tombs. These artefacts, and their relationship to the people who used and buried them, are the subject of the next chapter. Undeniably, they demonstrate at least a connection between the East and Etruscan Italy. The question is whether the objects were acquired by indigenous peoples, or whether they arrived with a new influx of settlers. In this scenario, it was these new arrivals who quickly overcame the makers of the hut-urns, and the first inhabitants at Tarquinia and other Etruscan settlements. The expansion of these population centres has also been used to argue for population change – the location of settlements may have stayed constant, but the growth and development of urban areas through the eighth and seventh centuries could be construed as the result of more sophisticated arrivals from regions already familiar with the concept of city living. The final shift in the archaeological evidence that could be used to support the Herodotus hypothesis is a dramatic change in the disposal of the dead. Cremation, whether in elaborate hut-urns or the more usual biconical urns (these get their name from their shape – an hourglass-like two cones on top of each other), begins to vanish at the same point in time that these imports arrive, the same moment that the fledgling towns and cities of Etruria expand. The dead are no longer burnt, but buried intact, with increasingly elaborate grave assemblages. Hut-urns go out of fashion, and elaborate tombs for entire corpses become the preferred form of burial for the wealthy.

The arrival of these three major changes – in materials, in settlement size and in the treatment of the dead – at first sight gives some weight to the suppositions of the ancient authors, in spite of their biases. Yet even within these supposedly watertight pieces of evidence for immigration, there are also signs of continuity. First, materials: Etruscan metalwork and pottery, while making use of Eastern motifs, also bears close resemblance to the locally made products found in burials like our urn. Fibulae (metal brooches used to pin clothing in place) are one set of objects which show continuity. Pottery fabrics, too, show clear development from the clays used to build this house urn. Second, as observed above, settlements remain in the same places, with presumably the same populations living within them. Looking at a site like Gran Casso, or Tarquinia, it seems unlikely in the extreme that a new group marched in and took over without establishing their own new towns. Allegiance to places, allegiance to ancestors: growth in the same locations is not evidence for large-scale population movement. And finally, while inhumation gradually became normalized, some aspects of the old ways survived. This is most notable in the retention of house-like features in tomb architecture, with beams like those on our urn carved into rock, and rich fabrics painted onto later tomb walls.[17] The continued dedication to cremation as a burial rite in some areas (notably inland, around the city of Chiusi) further undermines the idea of a new elite sweeping in with new ideas on how to deal with the dead.

The archaeological record from the ninth to seventh centuries BCE is, therefore, a bit of a conundrum, particularly when mixed up with the classical texts. The problem of Etruscan origins during this period neatly illustrates a central issue with investigating the deep past. You can line up 'facts' on either side of an argument;

you can use the evidence to build two entirely different answers to a question. If you give more weight to words then the archaeology can act as your crutch. If you privilege the material culture, you can accuse the texts of inaccuracy. In the history of Etruscan studies, the two sides of the debate have ebbed and flowed. Yet the preference for one point over another was itself defined by the cultural consciousness of the times in which the historians and archaeologists of the past were writing. The rediscovery of Etruscan culture was a painfully slow process, but its pace increased remarkably by vast excavations in the early nineteenth century. At this point, it seemed obvious to everyone that Herodotus was correct, and should be taken literally. George Dennis (1814–1898), who popularized Etruscan archaeology in Britain in the late nineteenth century, summarized the general view of scholars outside Italy: 'No fact can be more clearly established than the oriental character of the civic and religious polity, the social and domestic manners, and many of the arts of the Etruscans.' Dennis was writing to sell the Etruscans to an avid audience, and as a result some of his statements are hopeful in the extreme – for example, he describes the contents of Etruscan tombs as a 'second Pompeii'.[18] The intensity of opinion wrapped up in Dennis's prose makes his discussion of the origins argument particularly interesting. Steadily he wheeled out all the evidence available to support his model of Eastern origins. A snide little comment dismisses the idea of Etruscan culture as Italian in origin as mere nationalist drumbeating. The great Italian (indeed Tuscan) classical archaeologist Giuseppe Micali (1768–1864), who had died forty years previously, was the carefully chosen victim of Dennis's sneer.

Micali was certainly involved in the burgeoning Italian nationalist movement of the early nineteenth century, and the identity of the Etruscans as early Italians was important to the beliefs of this political group. Carlo Denina (1731–1813), historian and friend of Micali, placed the Etruscans at the centre of his history of Italy – a nation unconquered and independent, a league of city states brought together by their love of freedom.[19] Micali was not unaware of the connection between his beliefs about Italy's future and his study of her past, but in the face of criticism he maintained his view that Etruscan culture was authentically Italian. Prior to the unification of Italy as a nation, these ideas were provocative, even dangerous. After the Risorgimento of 1871, the Etruscans-as-Italians idea became even more important. As nationalist feeling swelled into the early twentieth century, so too did dedication to seeking evidence for the Etruscans as indigenous Italians. The joyful connection of Etruscan virtues with Italian ideals would turn sour, tarnished by association. For after Mussolini and his blackshirts marched on Rome in 1922, the argument over Etruscan origins would become a central part of fascist ideologies of the past.

Mussolini is best known for his self-identification with Roman, not Etruscan, ideals. His infatuation with the concept of *romanità* and his desire to build a second Roman Empire had disastrous consequences for Italy and continues to reverberate in the modern world. The humiliation of his campaigns in Ethiopia undermined his own mystique, in spite of a vigorous propaganda machine. Those affected by unrest in Libya and those fleeing the Eritrean regime are only the latest victims of this colonial misadventure, the inheritors of instability. While preferring to identify with the straightforward, bulldozing march of Rome, the Fascists also had designs on the Etruscan past. In 1922, the medieval town of Corneto was renamed Tarquinia, an exercise in resurrecting past prestige. While the renaming ceremony was an exquisite piece of Fascist theatre, it was in the universities that the effects of this obsession with Italian origins would appear. The classical scholar Giulio Quirino Giglioli (1886–1956) vehemently denied any connection with or influence from Greece and the Eastern Mediterranean.[20] As far as he was concerned, the Etruscans were, and always had been, an early example of Italian cultural supremacy. In this, Giglioli was bang on the message.

While the world prepared for war, a student of Giglioli called Massimo Pallottino was working hard on material from the earliest Etruscan period, including artefacts from Tarquinia. By 1939, Pallottino was ready to publish his analyses. The desire ignited by Fascist principles to prove the Italian origins of the Etruscans had resulted in an extraordinary piece of scientific analysis. Deliberately and carefully, Pallottino put forward the archaeological evidence

Sixth-century canopic cremation urn from Chiusi, a city where old burial customs refused to die.

for the Etruscans having their origins in Italy. He pieced together the connections – settlements, linguistics, artefacts. It was Pallottino who traced the development of ceramics and bronzes, who carefully drew out and plotted the shifting design of fibulae and razors, cups and jugs. More originally, and more dangerously, Pallottino criticized the dominant ideas that had prompted his work in the first place. The whole concept of set cultures represented by objects and based upon a solid definition of race was, to him, entirely inappropriate. While he was happy to accept that, fundamentally, the Etruscans were a home-grown phenomenon, Pallottino was furious at blind adherence to theory in the face of evidence. Here he is, risking his career on the brink of war: 'The majority of scholars do not concern themselves with a critical problem and present conclusions which are accepted without discussion.'[21] After the fall of Mussolini, Pallottino would go on to become the greatest Etruscan scholar of the twentieth century. Yet the argument over Etruscan origins, which he had done so much to elevate above dogmatic political belief, would stagnate. Inside Italy, Italian origins were accepted. Elsewhere, scholars continued to toy with the other ideas. The question drifted into stalemate, as archaeologists nervously steered away from identity politics, fingers burned from the conscription of the past into the ideologies that sparked the Second World War.

Yet in the late twentieth and early twenty-first century, the issue of Etruscan origins exploded back into life. This time, it wasn't nationalist sentiment that fuelled the resurgence. It was the rise of genetics, and the tempting idea of proving a point once and for all with the aid of deoxyribonucleic acid – DNA. The first attempt to use genetics to discuss Etruscan origins was in 1996, when a group of scientists looked at the genes of 49 modern Tuscans, and concluded that their DNA was about what you would expect – midway between the high variation of Near Eastern genes and the low variation of isolated Western European populations (Basques and Britons).[22] So far, so bland. In 2004, another study looked at DNA from Etruscan burials – a sample of eighty individuals, reduced to thirty due to the risk of contamination from modern sources.[23] The conclusions were equally unsurprising – the level of variation in the Etruscan remains was absolutely standard for a population sharing common ancestry. The results also showed that modern Tuscans were, by and large, not related to the thirty individual Etruscans whose genes had been sequenced; again, unsurprising given the degree of population shift over time. The DNA had barely moved the argument forward at all, but in 2007, the situation changed. Two teams of scholars came out strongly in favour of the Eastern origins argument. One had sequenced DNA from humans, the other from cows. Let's start with the cows.

One of the great pleasures of a trip to Florence is eating a piece of beef the size of your plate. Tender, delicious and expensive, beef from the Val di Chiana is a special treat. The cows that provide this *bistecca alla fiorentina* are charismatic beasts, pure white with sooty black noses. The breed, known as Chianina, is reckoned to be one of the most ancient in Europe, with a pure gene pool stretching back hundreds, if not thousands, of years. Along with ten other ancient Italian breeds, the Chianina cattle were subject to an in-depth genetic analysis with ramifications for the argument over Etruscan origins.[24] The scientists working on the cattle project sequenced the DNA of 164 different animals, which they then compared to the genetic make-up of other breeds from Europe and the Near East. The cattle formed groups of interrelated breeds, associated with particular origin points. The team suggested that the origin for the Chianina cattle, alongside the other Tuscan breeds, was Anatolia, with 60 per cent of the animals' mitochondrial DNA (that inherited from the female line) associated with other breeds from this region. A distinctive quirk in the DNA has been dated to have developed between the late Neolithic and the early Byzantine period – a wide range of time which includes the possible dates for Etruscan migrations. The assumption is that the Etruscans brought their favourite white cows from Lydia, loath to leave behind the top quality beef and attractive hides they had carefully developed in their cattle. The scientists suggested that this migration of people and animals took place during the Late Bronze Age, far earlier than Herodotus places the heroic journey of the Lydians to the West.

The data from the human subjects was also used to support the idea of the Eastern origins hypothesis for the Etruscans.[25]

For this study, mitochondrial DNA was taken from over three hundred living Tuscans, inhabitants of three towns with a link to the Etruscan past: Murlo, Volterra and the Casentino Valley. The results appeared conclusive – the individuals from Murlo in particular were different from other Italian samples, and even in Volterra and the Casentino Valley there were aspects of the DNA, or haplotypes, that were shared with Near Eastern populations but not with other Italians and Western Europeans. The media fell upon the conclusions with glee, presenting a favourite narrative of modern science overcoming messy archaeology. However, the study results are not quite so clear-cut. The results suggested that women with Near Eastern ancestry lived in all three places at some point between the Neolithic and the present day. This is a vast stretch of time, and the history of the Italian peninsula is one of mixing and movement – populations swirling around from the Neolithic through the Roman periods and into the medieval era. More significantly, of the eleven characteristics associated with the Near East that showed up in the Murlo samples, only one was specifically connected to Anatolia – the supposed origin point for Herodotus' Etruscans.

Both of these genetic studies had real problems.[26] The conclusion of the cattle study is hard to accept in light of the archaeological evidence – there really isn't a clear migration into Tuscany, even during the Late Bronze Age. While this time was a period of upheaval elsewhere in the Mediterranean (and this timing for Etruscan origins has even been linked to the fall of historical Troy in around 1200 BCE), is it likely that in the event of the war and famine in the Eastern Mediterranean that people would have diligently transported their cattle thousands of miles by sea? A far more convincing idea, given both the archaeological record and the practical realities of moving a significant population of intractable large bovines, is that the Chianina DNA reflects a careful breeding programme with far older roots, dating back to the original domestication of cattle in the Near East, not Turkey. These white cattle seem more like the descendants of a very early breed, brought under human control during the late Neolithic and transported overland to Italy. The original study authors had thought of this, and countered it, stating that domesticated animals seem to have spread from south to north through Italy, and that southern Italian breeds have a very different genetic signature. However, a larger investigation found evidence that supported multiple influxes of domestic cows into Italy during the millennia after their initial domestication.

This first set of human DNA studies might appear more convincing. They have certainly convinced the residents of Murlo, who will proudly declare their Etruscan heritage to you while enjoying a morning coffee at the village bar. The thing is that Murlo, and its delightful café bar, was not built on the site of an ancient Etruscan settlement. The neighbouring Etruscan site was abandoned in the fifth century BCE, and while there is evidence for Hellenistic and Roman occupation at the nearby village at the time of writing, there is no sense of settlement continuity. The village developed in response to the needs of the Bishops of Siena for a summer getaway, somewhere cool in the hills away from the intense heat of the episcopal palace. The community of servants, church officials and hangers-on that accompanied this secular pilgrimage were most likely the ancestors of today's residents, not an isolated band of Etruscan survivors. The issue of genetic continuity is even more damaging to the results from Volterra and the Casentino Valley, both places with their own disturbed histories of population movement and change.

These issues were pointed out by a large-scale restudy of the genetic data.[27] To eliminate these problems, a team of geneticists analysed DNA from three different populations: modern Tuscans (including the genes of the Murlo, Volterra and Casentino Valley residents taken seven years previously), medieval Tuscans and Etruscans. They included samples from Florence as a control, and compared their results to two 'standard' genetic signatures characteristic of Europe, and of the Near East. The inclusion of DNA from ancient populations set this study apart, allowing the scientists to establish whether connections did exist between Etruscans, modern and medieval Tuscans. Their results showed that the Florentines and Murlo residents were not related to the Etruscans in their sample. However, there were links with individuals at

Volterra and even more strongly at Casentino Valley. Excitingly, the team were able to establish connections with their Near Eastern sample – and to date these. The result was that the last shared ancestor between the Etruscan and Near Eastern individuals was found to have lived about 7,600 years ago. The ancestors of the Etruscans arrived in Italy during the Neolithic period. The evidence from this cohesive study fits with the data from the large cattle study. It also fits with the Neolithic archaeology, the Late Bronze Age archaeology and the Etruscan archaeology. It comprehensively does not fit with the classical sources and the Eastern origins hypothesis. Finally, after thousands of years of argument, it looks as though Herodotus was wrong, and the Italian nationalists were right.

Origins and migration remain current topics. The news remains dominated by harrowing images of desperate people spending vast amounts of money to escape violence, famine and economic disaster, but ending up risking their lives aboard leaking vessels in a stormy Mediterranean sea. A migration crisis, with Italy in particular struggling to manage the integration of new arrivals and find a strategy that saves lives but discourages people smugglers. The age-old story of the flight of the Etruscans from the East mirrors the modern situation, but Tyrrhenus and his followers would not receive the same reception today. The identity of the person buried in our Tarquinian urn has been recast again and again, each generation reinventing the story of Etruscan origins to suit its own preferences. In a time of population movement, uncertainty and change, even the seemingly conclusive results of the genetic study seem to reflect a separatist view of Etruscan origins, downplaying shared ancestry with the Near East. The question of Etruscan origins is, for now, settled. So where did the images and objects that led Dennis down the wrong track come from?

THREE

Ostrich Eggs and Oriental Dreams

Travelling north from Tarquinia, the landscape subtly shifts. You are edging towards the flat marshlands of the Maremma, and the coastal resorts vanish, replaced by scrubland. After the dramatic scarp rearing above the sea, these flatlands seem drab. Yet it is here that some of the most remarkable discoveries in Etruscan archaeology have taken place. The Etruscan city of Vulci, unlike Tarquinia, has not survived as a settlement. Long abandoned, the closest modern settlement is the small town of Montalto di Castro. On arrival at the Archaeological Park that covers the site, there's not much to see. Indeed, the first visible attraction is a herd of the white cattle discussed in the previous chapter. This does not appear to be the richest fount of Etruscan treasures, the home of spectacular artefacts, found in vast numbers. This set of fields, studded with grubby ruins – a sad Roman archway, half destroyed temples and numerous lumps and bumps – was the source of beautiful objects that have found homes in museums all over the world.

Approaching one of the mounds, you suddenly realize how much human effort has gone into creating it. The deep entranceway, known as a dromos, stretches downwards into the earth. On and on, you take each step carefully, stepping at last behind the glass door into the cool darkness of a burial place. Now it makes sense. This is a place where the dead were privileged, laid to rest amid the trappings of life, beneath tumuli raised by hundreds of hands, putting in the hours to demonstrate the power of dead ancestors and living families. You might be forgiven for thinking that the mound would be quite enough of a spectacle, enough to make a lasting impression. Yet inside these tombs were placed a range of goods that illustrate the wealth and power of some individuals in this society – a trading network that stretched for thousands of miles, access to resources that won items as valuable and exotic as any lottery winner could dream of. The objects at the centre of this chapter come from a single tomb within the Polledrara necropolis at Vulci. This tomb is only one of hundreds that encircle the city – there are four separate necropoleis, with the largest, Osteria, to the north of the settlement area. Polledrara, Ponte Rotto and Cavalupo are all to the east, studded with mounds and dips, still revealing treasures.[1]

The objects from this tomb are not to be found in the lonely museum at Vulci. They lie, cossetted by conservators and carefully lit, in the Etruscan gallery of the British Museum.[2] Crowds of schoolchildren dash past on their way to the showstoppers, the gilded mummies and shining Saxon treasures – if you are looking for a spot of peace and quiet among the hubbub of a visit, the Etruscan gallery is a good bet. It sits in a corner of the vast building, with sixty objects from this special tomb among other treasures from across Italy. The captions label each item; the lights bounce off bronze and faience (an early form of glass), ivory and clay. The story of these objects – their journey from the hands of the people who made them to burial in an Etruscan tomb through the hands of antiquities dealers to a safe haven in a backwater of the British Museum – is the story of this chapter.

So what are these special objects? Here are some of the artefacts found in this single burial:

- A bronze statue of a woman holding a gilded bird.
- A gold diadem, covered with designs of fantastical beasts and palms.
- Four ostrich eggs, carved with intricate patterns of horses and chariots.
- A series of bronze cups and bowls, some simple, some complicated.
- Three alabaster and gypsum perfume bottles, all formed in the shape of women.

Winged lion tomb guardian from a tumulus, or earthen mound, near Vulci, *c.* 550 BCE, stone sculpture (nenfro). Was its design inspired by contact with the Near East?

- A group of terracotta spools, which may have once held rich threads.
- A bronze lamp and lamp stand.
- A group of amulets in the shape of dung beetles.
- Five shining flasks made of faience.
- A painted gypsum statue of a woman with outstretched hands.

Any of these objects would make for a spectacular find. The cache of spools, the ostrich eggs – any one of these finds would be the highlight of an archaeological career. Together, as an assemblage – a deliberately curated collection of objects – they are incredible.[3] The people who placed these objects together had access not only to the very best of Etruscan workmanship in the form of the bronze sculptures and vessels, but to the most luxurious objects that the ancient Mediterranean had to offer. The dung beetle amulets, or scarabs, are a good place to start. These industrious little creatures, rolling their balls of faeces across the desert sands, are ineffably associated with one place: Egypt. The carved eggs could have come from Egypt too, defunct offspring of the now-endangered North African ostrich. Yet the carving is a style familiar from the archaeology of the Near East, and the scarabs too suggest an origin in the Levant. The carved alabaster perfume vessel was made in western Turkey, probably in a community of people who considered themselves Greek.

If you only found one of these objects, you might think that the person buried with it had brought that object across the seas themselves, perhaps a migrant. With the classical texts echoing in your head, the Turkish perfume vessels might suggest you had found some concrete evidence to support the Herodotus story. The problem is that the people buried in this tomb weren't just accompanied by *one* of these stand-out objects – they received the whole lot. So the conviction that objects define where a person comes from becomes hard to sustain. It's approximately 1,250 miles to the Egyptian coast from Vulci; it is around 1,000 miles to western Turkey, and 1,400 miles to the shores of Syria and Lebanon. Unless the people buried in this tomb were a mixture of individuals from all these different places, each buried with the best their craftspeople could produce, we are seeing the fruits of a trading network that stretched across these thousands of miles, along with some of the remarkable goods that provided for their purchase in the first place.

This point in time, the late seventh century BCE, was the culmination of over a hundred years of social change.[4] Burial practice shifted towards the great mounds, away from urns and flames. Towns grew out of villages, as people settled in increasing numbers around central attractions – places to trade, places to share beliefs, places to meet and share.[5] This process of change is only slightly interrupted during the first half of the seventh century – a point at which this growth seems to falter. The burgeoning early centres began to contract. It is tempting to look for environmental factors to find the causes for this recession. Perhaps a series of bad harvests, or a wobble in climate, led to the famously fertile Tuscan soil failing the people who relied upon it for their living – although there's little to no evidence for this in studies of the period. Or the mechanisms for bringing in wealth failed – perhaps the metal resources that made Etruria rich dwindled for a while, until new sources were found. It was surely these two sources of bounty – the metallic ores and fertile soils – that enabled the inhabitants of central Italy to surge forward once again during the second half of the seventh century, leaping back to prominence and wealth. It was at this point that the artefacts found in our tomb were assembled.

Ostrich egg decorated with sphinxes, from the Isis tomb, Vulci.

A perfume vessel imported from Naukratis, Egypt, to Tarquinia, 6th century.

What was it about these designs, these materials, that made them so popular and so precious? The idea of exoticism, that objects are valuable due to their distant origins, has been the traditional reason given for their appeal. This idea has uncomfortable connotations. The conception of exotic is tainted, forever associated with either zoos and gawping, or worse, with colonialism and exploitation. Eighteenth- and nineteenth-century models of trade recall the arrival in European and American cities of people, objects and animals from the furthest reaches of Empire, valued for their strangeness, the otherness that brought together those who viewed them. On the other side of the coin, traders could look down on indigenous communities who they steadily short-changed, using the mystique of faraway materials to manipulate them.[6] In the modern globalized world, the value of distance has disappeared from objects. 'Made in China', 'Made in Taiwan' – the faraway location of an object's production no longer possesses an emotional pull. The container ship and the factory floor have removed exoticism from the everyday encounter.

Or have they? Exotic still exists, but in a different form. Recognizing what makes a modern object special provides an insight into a desire shared with the Etruscan inhabitants of Vulci. It is not distance but relationships that make an object special. It is exactly the impersonal nature of modern long-distance trades that has sapped their power to thrill. Instead, it is the people we have met, the stories we can tell, that give a thing its value. Even an ordinary item – a loaf of bread – becomes extraordinary once it is elevated by personal relationships. The relationships that make this bread special extend outwards in two directions from the person doing the serving: guests appreciate that their host has the right kind of connections; the bakery owners gain new audiences. The host can brag of their links to the bakery, or choose not to – the bread will do the talking.

It's easy to be facetious, to make fun of the hipster ideal of the personalized commodity. It was also easy to trot out the mileage of each item found in the tomb. Yet it is not the miles themselves that define these artefacts as exotic, as valuable. It is the connections and links that cross the miles that are so impressive. Each object represents a series of journeys made on a purchaser's behalf, links in a chain that crossed the seas. Whether or not they were acquired from trading settlements established by Near Eastern and Greek migrants in Sicily and Sardinia, or gained on direct missions to Egypt, Turkey and the Levant, though interesting, is not vitally important. Such objects were symbols that their owners were plugged in to an impressive and valuable chain of relationships.[7] They had the right connections, were part of a trans-Mediterranean elite, able to impress at home with their links to the world beyond. The archaeological evidence for the existence of these shared values is scattered all over the trade routes these people were plugged into. Shipwrecks off the coast of Turkey have been found to contain jewellery from Sardinia and bronzes from Etruria.[8] The objects in the tomb at Vulci are the material remains of a social network, with people liking and sharing both physical things and ideals. These ideals are reflected in the objects themselves – rich oils and luxurious threads, for making the body beautiful; drinking sets of costly bronze, dedicated to transforming eating and drinking into a special experience. From shore to shore, people were trading on their shared value of pleasure. Showing off who you knew, what your wealth and position could buy you from them, and the fun of what you received – what's not to enjoy?

This list of items is only a fraction of the artefacts buried in the tomb, however. An unknowable number of other items were smashed to pieces by the discoverers. For this tomb was excavated in the early nineteenth century, ransacked by treasure hunters who stumbled upon a glimmering hoard. It was the imported objects that caught their eye, far more than the locally made goods. Just as the staggering connections impress modern visitors, it was the link with the East that the discoverers seized upon. The perceived influence attached to the goods gave its name to this entire period of Etruscan history – it was termed Orientalizing. The fascination of the Orient, a mystical land inhabited by a strange and dangerous Other, had a deep pull over European audiences for centuries. This idea, described and critiqued by the philosopher Edward Said, was mired in colonial insecurity and racial bias.[9] Myths and tales, from *The Arabian Nights* to the stories of Rudyard Kipling, all shared in the making of this legend. It is the same narrative that lies behind the lost civilization myth, as described in the Prologue to this book. Inevitably, the materials from Vulci were sucked into the story, part of a deliberate opposition of East and West, Europe and Asia. Perhaps this was unavoidable, given the identity of the man who funded their discovery in the first place.

Lucien Bonaparte (1775–1840) was a highly fortunate young man.[10] Born into relative poverty in Corsica, the third of eight children, the stratospheric rise of his brother Napoleon had transformed his destiny. Unlike some of the other Bonaparte siblings, however, Lucien was deeply unsettled by his brother's power. A genuine believer in the revolutionary cause, Lucien became president of the lower house of the French revolutionary parliament, the Council of Five Hundred, only to be ousted by his brother's coup in 1799. Storming into the parliamentary chambers, Napoleon forcibly disbanded the Council. Lucien threatened to kill his brother if he betrayed the revolutionary principles of *liberté, égalité, fraternité*. This was a piece of showboating designed to reassure onlookers of the family's dedication to the Republic. However, real cracks had already begun to appear in this fraternal united front by 1800, after seditious pamphlets were traced back to Lucien's hand. In spite of the growing distrust between the siblings, Napoleon dispatched Lucien to Spain, where he won over the Bourbon royal family to his brother's cause. On his return, however, the relationship between the two men steadily deteriorated.

The last straw for Lucien was the attempt by Napoleon to force him into a dynastic marriage with the widowed Queen of Etruria. He fled to Rome in 1804, moving into a luxurious villa in the beautiful wine-growing town of Frascati. It was this move that piqued Lucien's archaeological interests. Near to Frascati are the ruins of the city of Tusculum, and Lucien began excavations on his lands, discovering a remarkable Imperial statue of the emperor Tiberius. Ten years later, after a flight to England, Lucien returned to Italy and to his passion for the past. He was enthroned as Prince of Canino by the Pope in 1814, while Napoleon was exiled in Elba. This title brought with it lands in the province of Viterbo – including a certain village known as Montalto di Castro. It was towards the end of his life, in 1839, that he sponsored a team to begin work in the Polledrara Cemetery. While Lucien had opened Etruscan tombs before, this excavation was a spectacular success.[11] The glorious gypsum statue of a woman was immediately (and wrongly) identified with the Egyptian goddess Isis, and the tomb given its enduring name – the Isis tomb.

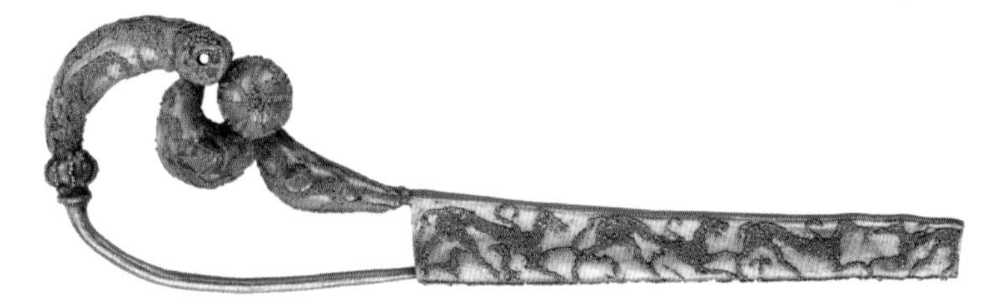

Fibula with granulated decoration – a favourite Etruscan technique – from the 7th century.

Small skyphos, or drinking cup, 6th century BCE.

This identification links with a key moment in the development of the 'Orientalizing' period as an idea. The direct connection of the tomb to the Bonaparte family is important too. For the label of the Orient, and the fantasy of the East into which Etruscan culture was slotted, was largely defined by Lucien's brother's most famous conquests – in Egypt and the Levant. Napoleon had begun warming up the French establishment to the idea of taking power in Egypt in 1798, seeing it as an opportunity to disrupt British involvement in India. His ideas were enthusiastically received – the scheme was seen as a way of removing a potentially dangerous political rival from France. If successful, it would simultaneously damage Britain and boost the fragile economy of the Republic. French and Italian forces embarked at ports across the Mediterranean in May 1789. Over forty thousand men disembarked at Alexandria on 1 July, followed by Napoleon on his flagship *L'Orient*. In spite of the vicious heat, the army progressed southwards, taking Cairo after a fierce battle within sight of the pyramids at Giza.

The victorious Napoleon deliberately began to emulate the city's elite, determined to present himself as a liberator and a friend of Islam. This act failed to convince the Egyptian population. By October, Cairo was in revolt. Vicious street fighting ended with Napoleon ordering the firing of the Grand Mosque, an act of terror which cowed the city. Ruling by fear, Napoleon felt safe enough to expand his offensive northeastwards, marching on through Sinai to Palestine. He took control of the lands as far as the Gaza Strip, before being turned back by British naval forces and the Ottoman army. A year on from the initial venture eastwards, 600 men had been lost to disease, 1,200 killed in battle and 1,800 wounded. Napoleon left Egypt for power in France in August 1799, leaving behind a military mire. Britain would take Egypt only scant years later, assisted by the alienated Egyptian Mameluke rulers who had seen through Napoleon's cultural appropriation.[12]

Napoleon's army had been accompanied by a group of scholars determined to conquer Egypt's past, as well as its present. These scholars personified the importance of Orientalism as a scientific concept. They illustrated the supposedly essential features of Egyptian and Levantine life. Passive acceptance of outside authority, cultural stasis, the luxurious lives of a corrupt elite – these characteristics were used to illustrate the superiority of French values. It is not a coincidence that these social ills exactly reflected the evils of the last days of the French monarchy. At the same time, the French (but also the British, Germans and, as we saw in Chapter Two, the Italians) laid claim to the inheritance of the classical world. Re-imagined through an Enlightenment lens, classical rationalism, republicanism, democracy – all were embraced by politicians and thinkers delighted by the idea of themselves as heirs to the glories of Rome and Greece.[13] The die was cast: Eastern indolence against Western self-determination. This racist pseudoscience, designed to back up a series of usurpations of land and power in the Near East and Asia, trickled into the archaeological endeavours of the expedition, even as it dictated public opinion of the Ottoman realms back in France. The splendours of ancient Egypt embodied dynastic rule, with its spectacular inequalities and equally spectacular artefacts. By bringing Egyptian antiquities back to France, the people would be introduced to authoritarian ancient rulers through their works.

That was the intention of Napoleon's army of archaeological pirates, raiding Egypt's ancient sites. It did not quite play out as originally planned, however. After Napoleon abandoned his campaign to return to France and seize power, his scientists were left struggling with their vast collections. In 1801, the vast majority of the objects were seized by the British Navy and shipped back to Britain. The objects included the iconic Rosetta Stone, and became the founding Egyptian collection of the British Museum. There they were used to introduce the same sense of cultural separation in London as they had been intended for in Paris. The story of Napoleon's lost antiquities chimes with the fate of the finds from Lucien's excavations. Four years after Lucien Bonaparte's death in 1840, the same fate befell his collection from the Isis tomb. His widow, in need of ready funds, sold sixty items to the German archaeologist Emil Braun, who in turn sold them to the British Museum. Just as the British public could ogle the fruits of despotic rule in Egypt, they were also free to gaze at objects that transported this dangerous Eastern influence to the very doorstep of Rome.

The concepts of Orientalism honed through Napoleon's campaign in Egypt were brought to bear on the antiquities his brother unearthed from Vulci. Identified with Egypt through the female statue, the artefacts became part of a perhaps less conscious narrative – that of the pernicious influence of the East on pre-Roman Italy. The study and display of these artefacts were initially seen as proof of the veracity of the classical sources dealing with the origin myth of the Etruscans.[14] Even after this idea was dispelled by the archaeology in the early twentieth century, the taint of the Oriental clung to this period of rapid development and change. The inequality inherent in the acquisition of such luxury goods was characterized as associated with authoritarian rule – the establishment of a system of kings. The Isis tomb, and others like it, were described in this language. They were 'princely' tombs, burial spaces of rulers cast in the image of pharaohs and maharajas.[15] The Etruscan Orientalizing period inherited the propaganda of Napoleon's campaign, and British fantasies of India. The Isis tomb, and others like it, became the burial places of kings and queens, princes and princesses, stuffed with inherited wealth.

The problem is that there is no evidence at all for this kind of rule in Italy. Yes, social inequality is made increasingly visible by the introduction of new goods from faraway places, but it seems far more likely that existing powerful families took advantage of their connections and holdings to establish trading empires rather than hereditary kingdoms.[16] New research is revealing the tiny proportion of objects from this period which were imported from the Eastern Mediterranean.[17] While objects *influenced* by Eastern designs – like those showing goddesses surrounded by wild beasts, and non-native animals such as lions – are represented more widely, they too make up a minimal proportion of the material culture of Etruscan society at this point. So not only do we have no evidence for princes, and little to no evidence for a migration from the East, we now have evidence that the scale of Eastern influence has been vastly over exaggerated. The artefacts that did arrive must have been incorporated into a largely independent system of beliefs and values, signs that marked out their owners as part of a trading network but not necessarily as rulers and leaders by hereditary right. The old Oriental model of rule in Etruria, based on the idea that the adoption of objects equals the adoption of ideas, is no longer a tenable idea.

The whole story of the objects from the Isis tomb, the development of an Orientalizing period and its downfall, is woven from a number of themes: the hubris of colonialism and the fear of the unknown, the equation of people with things and equation of wealth with royal power, the destruction of the everyday and preservation of the unusual. These are all features that continue to define our world. The after-effects of Orientalism as an attitude are perhaps more visible than ever. The Arab Spring was built upon the overthrow of dictators cast as Oriental despots, cheered on by a rationalist liberal media. Yet its aftershocks have resulted in the re-establishment of a self-declared caliphate, a political and military force that defines itself against the West. The fighters of so-called Islamic State (ISIS) have turned the racism of Oriental prejudice on its head, setting up Europe and America as Others in their turn. Their war on the West incorporates antiquities just as Napoleon's campaigns did. Instead of collecting and preserving, however, objects from the ancient past are seen as items for sale, or ideal fodder for propaganda videos. The sites and objects that defined Orientalist archaeology have become idols to be used to distance the forces of ISIS from their past. Examples of items similar to those found in the Isis tomb have been smashed and stolen, sold on an open market to vanish into private collections. Made in the Near East, they have become hostages in a war of ideas. Sat in their glass cases, the fragile ostrich eggs and delicately carved statues from the Isis tomb emphasize the consequences of imposing colonial worldviews on both the past and the present.

The story of these objects' impact on Etruscan archaeology has another lesson to teach us, namely not to associate people with objects. In an increasingly globalized world, things pass from culture to culture, being reinvented and reformed in the blink of an eye. Images and styles change and shift more and more quickly, lapped up by dedicated followers of fashion. Claiming identity through the origin of objects is increasingly problematic, and not just for archaeologists. It is what we as users *do* with things that is important. It is the way that objects allow us to make friends, claim kinship, share love, inspire respect. The goods from the Isis tomb, impressive though their disparate starting points might seem, survived because of the impression they made on their *owners'* lives. As a tool of communication, they are still shouting their message of wealth and connections as loudly as when they were first buried. Made by one pair of hands, passing through others and ending in a

Elaborate bronze cauldron, probably from Vetulonia, made in the early 7th century.

tomb, these remarkable objects are probably not the unique crown jewels of an Oriental-style autocratic royal dynasty, but the fruits of a lifetime of trade and exchange, carefully collected and brought together by a grieving family to make a statement about their lost loved ones. How and why they chose to do so is the subject of the next chapter.

FOUR
Pots and Prejudice

Objects like the Chiusi pot from Athens, on the next page, are part of the show-stoppers of any museum collection. Almost ubiquitous, yet still imbued with meaning, they sit behind glass as fragile pieces of art. They are indelibly associated with a single city and a single culture – and that culture is not Etruscan. Greek vases are fixed in our memories from childhood. We make wobbly drawings and awkward collages of their more sanitized scenes for classroom displays, goggle at their eroticism and boldness as teenagers, and bask in their cultural achievement as self-satisfied adults. They are undoubtedly compelling things, fragile bits of clay that have been grabbing attention for millennia. The problem is, the vast majority of these fabulous artefacts were not found in Greece.[1] In Athens, the city in which so many of them were made, they largely survive as fragments, bits and pieces uncovered in excavations beneath the modern city. The largely intact examples that fill us with awe were not found in Greece, but in Italy. In Etruria, to be precise.

Vases from Etruria filled up the collections of the Vatican, before being sold in the antiquities markets of Rome to museums and collectors across the world. Our particular pot, however, had a longer journey. After its arrival in Etruria, probably through the trading ports of Populonia, Gravisca or Pyrgi, this vase travelled inland; by road or by river, it travelled 175 km from the Tyrrhenian Sea. The city of Chiusi is very different from Tarquinia or Vulci. It lies on a high hill on the border between the modern provinces of Tuscany and Umbria. The region is defined by a string of volcanic

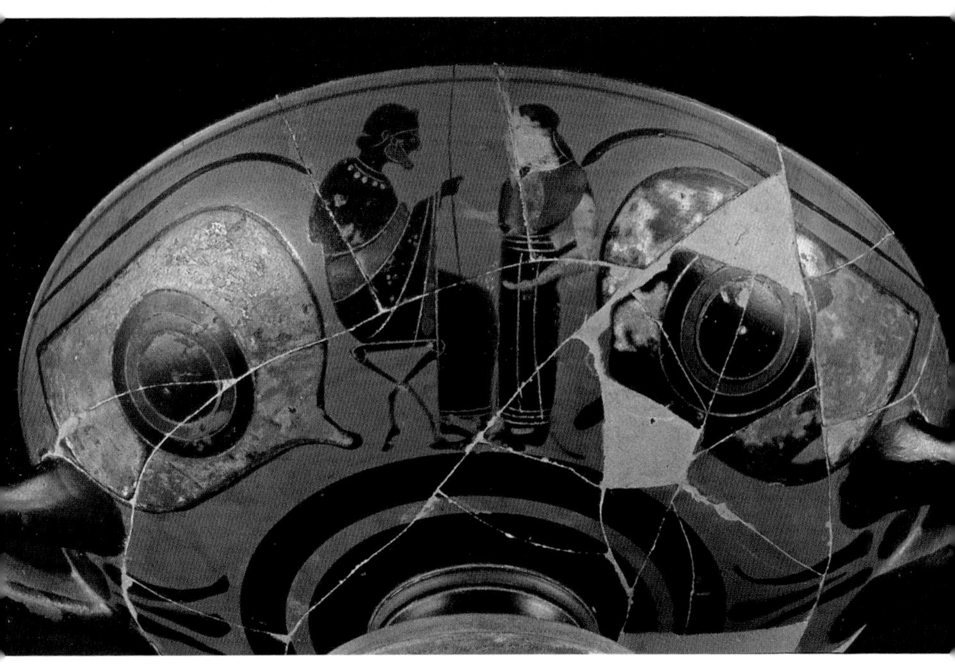

Kylix, or drinking cup, imported from Athens and buried in a tomb at Chiusi.

lakes, which shimmer on the horizon when you look out from the town in the heat of summer. Outside the town are some scruffy looking mounds covered in trees. If you can find them, you can carefully walk along some of the faint pathways that survive over them, but watch your step. These mounds are hollowed out with passageways and vaults. There is a medieval legend that an Etruscan king of Chiusi built a labyrinth to rival that of Knossos, and it certainly feels that way when exploring these strange chambers cut into the earth.

From looking at these burial places, you would never imagine that something so delicate could survive within them. Yet survive it did, to end up carefully and lovingly displayed in the city museum. In recent years, the museum's exhibitions have been beautifully redesigned. The glass cases are organized chronologically, and you wander around in a large circle, beginning with the earliest Iron Age material. At the end are the enduringly appealing late-Etruscan portrait urns, topped with portly aristocrats looking miffed at eternal life. The vase dates to midway between these two moments in time, to the heyday of the Etruscan cities. It was made between the years 520 and 510 BCE. Like the objects from the Isis tomb, the vase was excavated in the nineteenth century. Unlike them, it was unearthed not as part of a ducal project, but as a consequence of some transformative technology. The railway line that runs through Chiusi is the main line from Florence to Rome, and it was by train that the first antiquarians arrived in the town.[2] The museum is stuffed with their discoveries, but other artefacts were whisked away down the line to the antiquities markets in Rome or Florence. In particular, artefacts of value, like this one.

Unfortunately, this vase is partly broken, with chunks missing. It is not as imposing as other examples, as it was probably damaged during excavation. It is a drinking cup, flat and wide, not a haughty amphora used for pouring the wine. It is absolutely typical of its kind, red and black, with highlights in white. Those highlights are a strangely shaped pair of non-attached eyes, and the skin of a woman's body. She stands before a bearded man, who is seated on what looks uncannily like a camp stool. He holds a sceptre, or a staff. She stands with both arms outstretched, in a pose that calls to mind bargaining, or the illustration of her words with an emphatic gesture. On the inside of the cup is a grinning gorgon. The man and woman are more serious. The disembodied eyes just seem strange. All together, however, the cup and its decorations have a compelling beauty: the delicate lines with which the man's cloak and woman's dress are etched, the swooping shapes of the eyes, the twirl in the gorgon's beard hairs – this image was obviously made by skilled artisans, even artists. They are the product of a 'high' culture.

The set of ideas imbued within this vase have a long history. The first recorded discovery of black- and red-figure vases like this one took place just up the railway line from Chiusi, in the city of Arezzo. In 1284 the city's governors made the decision to rebuild its protective wall. The first job was to dig foundations, and the diggers hit upon what must have been an Etruscan burial. A monk from the city, Ristoro d'Arezzo, chronicled his impression that the objects had been sent by God as a sign to the city of Arezzo.[3] He described them as a special blessing from the Almighty. Over the course of the following centuries, the great powers in Tuscany became deeply interested in such artefacts. The notorious Medici family, de facto rulers of Florence from the fifteenth century, were voracious collectors of all forms of art.[4] While the display of Etruscan antiquities chimed with their claims of an ancient right to rule, such discoveries were also treated as art objects, things of beauty and wonder. In the collections of the greatest Medici rulers, Cosimo, first Grand Duke of Tuscany (1519–1574), and the Medici Pope Leo X (1475–1521), Etruscan artefacts sat side by side with works by the most talented artists of the Renaissance.[5] A remarkable sculpture of a bronze chimera, also discovered in Arezzo in the mid-sixteenth century, was restored under Cosimo's direction by the artist Cellini (1500–1571). The fragility of the vases, their elaborate and detailed painted decoration, ensured that they too crossed the divide between museum curiosity and artistic masterpiece.

Red- and black-figure vases continued to pop up at intervals during chance excavations and flirtations with archaeology. Two hundred years on from the passions of Cosimo and Leo, who had elevated archaeology to art, an intense interest in the Etruscans would re-emerge in Italy. In 1757, a landowner near Volterra, Mario Guarnacci, established a public museum, introducing the finds on his property to ordinary people.[6] Just as Etruscan artefacts were being opened up to the public, so too were previous studies of their history. A Scottish scholar, Thomas Dempster (1579–1625), had written an opus on Etruscan culture for Cosimo II de' Medici. It was republished for a popular Italian audience in 1723, funded by Thomas Coke (1697–1759), an Englishman enamoured of Italy during the course of his Grand Tour. Between the display of artefacts and the availability of printed information, the Etruscans were the height of fashion.

The Italians term this period of interest as 'Etruscheria', which can be loosely translated as 'Etruscomania'. It was not confined to Italy, however. Thomas Coke brought Etruscan artefacts back to England with him, and his home in Norfolk became a shrine to their beauty. Vases were also imported to England by Sir William Hamilton, the British ambassador in Naples, and he regularly sent

Cover of *De Etruria regali*, the book whose rediscovery launched Etruscomania.

THOMÆ
DEMPSTERI
A MURESK SCOTI
Pandectarum in Piſano Lyceo Profeſſoris Ordinarii
DE
ETRURIA REGALI
LIBRI SEPTEM
Opus Poſtumum
IN DUAS PARTES DIVISUM
Tomus Secundus
Poſteriores quatuor Libros comprehendens.

FLORENTIÆ. M.DCC.XXIII.
TYPIS REGIÆ CELSITUDINIS
Apud Joannem Cajetanum Tartinium, & Sanctem Franchium
CUM APPROBATIONE.

descriptions of new discoveries to the Society of Antiquaries back in London after taking up his post in 1760. 'Etruscan' rooms began to appear in the houses of the rich. Osterley Park, a neo-classical mansion in Hounslow, preserves an Etruscan-styled room, complete with elaborate images of themes from Etruscan art. Its designers, the Adam brothers, also installed Etruscan-themed decorative schemes in Home House, London, and Syon House, a vast mansion also in London. However, perhaps the most extreme example of Etruscomania in England was the obsession of the potter Josiah Wedgwood. He commissioned the design of a series of pots inspired by the supposedly Etruscan vases. Wedgwood even named his classical mansion, completed in 1771, Etruria Hall, and his factory Etruria Works. Above the factory gates was embossed the legend 'Artes Etruriae Renascuntur', declaring to all that 'The arts of the Etruscans are reborn!'

An idealized image of Johann Winckelmann, by Angelika Kaufmann, 1764, oil on canvas.

The problem was that it was not the arts of the Etruscans that were being reborn, but the arts of their contemporaries across the sea in Athens. The realization that an awful mistake had been made was not long in coming. A young German scholar, Johann Joachim Winckelmann (1717–1768), was about to end forever mainstream interest in the Etruscans. Winckelmann's career contrasts to that of

Coke. A cobbler's son, he did not have the wherewithal to finance a luxurious Grand Tour, in spite of his passion for the classical world. Instead, Winckelmann first studied theology, then changed course and trained to be a doctor, before dropping out to earn his living teaching. He quickly turned to private tutoring, taking advantage of his employers' aristocratic connections to go on and secure a position in charge of the library of Count Heinrich von Bünau. It was in this capacity that in 1755 he published his first book, arguing that the only way to achieve artistic excellence was to look back to the classical ideal. While this first work, translated as *Reflections on the Painting and Sculpture of the Greeks*, was not published in English until 1765, it was translated into French and transformed Winckelmann into one of Europe's leading intellectuals.[7] As a result of his new-found fame he was granted a pension that allowed him at long last to travel to Rome.

Winckelmann arrived in Rome late in 1755. He fell in with the intellectual circles of the city, and commenced his first task, analysing the sculptural techniques on display in the Cortile del Belvedere in the heart of the Vatican (after first converting to Catholicism). Still used as a gallery, when Winckelmann arrived the great court was filled with impressive classical sculptures, some of which today still bear the Belvedere name. Winckelmann was in ecstasy at the beauty of the masculine figures on show. His sojourn in Rome lasted rather longer than originally planned, thanks to the Seven Years War of 1756–63. As a result, his examination of the city's classical art was far more detailed. Each sculpture or vase was subjected to minute scrutiny, with the definition of a muscle or lilt of an eye recorded and set in place. Gradually, Winckelmann realized that many classical sculptures were Roman copies of earlier Greek examples – it was the Greeks, not the Romans, who had achieved what he saw as the ultimate artistic triumph. At the same time, he was also taking advantage of the opportunity to study the Vatican's other antiquities – from Egypt, and from Etruria, using the same techniques to consider the stylistic details of what he considered to be lesser artists. A visit to the excavations at Pompeii confirmed his opinion of the position of Roman painting and sculpture in his artistic pantheon.

Winckelmann put his observations together in his masterpiece, *The History of the Art of Antiquity*.[8] Published in 1764, it remains a compelling read, filled with pithy asides and characteristic vehemence. It was this work, more than any other, that toppled the idea of the Etruscans as creators of black- and red-figure vases. One volume is entirely dedicated to the Etruscans – and more particularly, to their relationship with his beloved Greeks.[9] That relationship is made clear in the very first volume, in which Winckelmann introduces his project, comparing Greek art with that of the Egyptians, Romans and Etruscans. Naturally, it is superlative. He revels in lyrical metaphors – Egyptian art is like a toppled

Made in Etruria: a Caeretan hydria showing the defeat of the hydra by Ercle (Herakles), attributed to the Eagle Painter, *c.* 525 BCE.

tree, cut down before it can develop; Etruscan art like a raging stream.[10] The art of classical Greece, by contrast, is compared to a beautiful river winding through a green valley, a vision of heaven. It is characterized, for Winckelmann, by the utmost simplicity of line, the representation of reality without exaggeration or understatement (the fatal flaws of indigenous Etruscan and Egyptian art respectively).

These features, which Winckelmann first identified in Greek sculpture, also define the style of painting seen on our vase from Chiusi. By comparing the images on the vases to those from Etruscan tombs, and from Etruscan metalwork and sculpture, he could see that the two styles of representation just did not fit together. To Winckelmann, it was entirely obvious that they were made in Greece and transported to Italy. But why would the Etruscans, with their own style of art, have wanted to import images from another people? For Winckelmann, the answer was straightforward – the Greeks had 'civilized the barbarous Etruscans'.[11] All Etruscan art was a poor copy of the Greek ideal, imported for its aesthetic appeal. The vases brought the complexities of Greek mythology to Italy, as well as the perfect way to represent the human form in two dimensions. The Etruscan interpretation of these myths, and the attempts of Etruscan artists to emulate imported materials, showed these well-meaning barbarians trying and failing to overcome their base nature. The Etruscans were bright enough to recognize the Greek genius – but not able to replicate it.

Winckelmann's views were incorporated into publications in English long before his *History of the Art of Antiquity* was belatedly translated in 1855. Sir William Hamilton was no longer content to simply report back to the Society of Antiquaries, instead organizing the publication of a catalogue of his ceramic treasures.[12] Pierre d'Hancarville (1719–1805), a Frenchman resident in Naples and a leading figure in the local antiquities market, was commissioned to bring Hamilton's collection to the reading (and paying) public. It was within the pages of this volume that Winckelmann's recognition of black- and red-figure vases as Greek was first proposed to an English-speaking audience. Gradually, inevitably, he was acknowledged to be correct. Etruscomania

A rather jolly sea monster demonstrating that Etruscan craftspeople occasionally struggled with their oeuvres.

was over. Nobody wanted to be associated with a second-rate civilization, a people defined by their magpie-like ability to take another culture's treasures while learning nothing from them. The Etruscan tombs where so many of the vases had been found became an inconvenient truth. From this point on, studies of these objects would focus on their connection with Greece, highlighting the techniques of their makers, and their relationship with Greek, not Etruscan, society.[13]

Etruscan archaeology was defined by this moment. The judgement of Winckelmann, echoed by other eminent scholars of this formative age, consigned the study of the Etruscans to a relative backwater of classical discourse. The lack of Etruscan texts compounded the problem: it seemed more appropriate to take the Etruscans at their more talented contemporaries' valuation. That valuation was a poor one. Quite apart from Herodotus' tale linking the ancestors of the Etruscans to the Persian enemy, other descriptions of the relationship between Greeks and Etruscans are telling. One particularly popular myth, first written down in the Homeric 'Hymn to Dionysus', describes the kidnap of a young man by Etruscan pirates.[14] While this young man turns out to be the wine god in disguise, the implication is that other victims of kidnapping and piracy were not so fortunate. The Etruscans on the high seas are portrayed as a threat to Greek interests and shipping, and go against the gods of Olympus – a sure sign of barbarism, which is duly punished as Dionysus turns his captors to dolphins.

The underlying threat posed by Etruscan sea power flared into violence between 540 and 535 BCE, when an allied force of Etruscans and Carthaginians fought a naval battle with Greek settlers. The Greek author Herodotus describes the triumph of their outnumbered forces, although the outcome of this Battle of Alalia somewhat favoured the allies.[15] Etruscan traders retained their foothold in Corsica, while the Carthaginians kept control of Sardinia. The journey of ceramics from Greece to Italy passed right through these troubled waters, and the battles fought over these trade routes emphasize just how valuable they were. The aggression between Greek and Etruscan traders and the propaganda dismissing Etruscan sailors as pirates implies a serious threat to Greek dominance in the Mediterranean. From the viewpoint of a passionate scholar immersed in Greek art, however, these actions were those of savages, an axis of evil threatening civilization. The combination of Winckelmann's depiction of the Etruscans as incapable of artistic originality and technical excellence with these reports of violence created an impression of a base people, which remains influential.[16]

The question of what Attic vases were traded *for* has also contributed to the prejudice against Etruscan owners of Greek pots. The idea that it was natural resources that were traded for cultural riches, Etruscan metal ores for Greek art, is a problematic one.[17] If Etruscan trading success was based solely on the luck of the lands they lived in, it can be dismissed. A further virtue for the Greeks: to have established themselves as trade masters based on scrubby dry land through their cultural endeavours. This vision of an unequal trade has echoes in later, colonial exchanges. It is a scenario that is deeply unethical, morally uncomfortable, but from the viewpoint of a colonially influenced scholar, entirely rational. The more 'developed' group exploits the weaker under a veil of civilizing influence. The savage Etruscans gave up the riches of

Attic vase imported to Tarquinia, showing Dionysus, Ariadne and attendant satyrs and maenads.

their lands to better use, receiving the glories of Greek art to raise them up in exchange.

The idea of colonial-style power relations between Greeks bearing gifts and Etruscans bearing base metals is beginning to appear outdated. Etruscan traders are recorded as having bases in the Eastern Mediterranean, hawking their wares from the island of Lemnos in particular.[18] Near the Greek colony of Massilia, now Marseilles, Etruscan trading settlements flourished.[19] In Spain, too, Etruscans were setting up shop and making new connections, tapping in to a wide range of products to bring home to Italy or sell for a profit elsewhere.[20] Even in Greece itself, Etruscan-made bronzes are to be found – not least in the great museum at Olympia. Trading with Greek city-states, Gauls in southern France and the Iberians of southern Spain, as well as with the great North African city of Carthage, Etruscan ships would have been able to command rich cargoes wherever they landed. It seems most likely

Etruscan helmet of the 4th century BCE; many similar examples are to be found at Olympia.

Nikosthenic amphora signed by the man himself, *c.* 520 BCE, showing a pair of boxers and a crouching youth.

that these merchants travelled with a mixture of goods on board – both raw materials and finished products.

If we accept this shift in interpretation of Greek–Etruscan trade relations, and look again at the pots themselves, it seems likely that the relationship between potters and painters in Athens and purchasers in Etruria was one between discerning clients and artful designers. At the same time as Attic wares became popular in Etruria, Etruscan shapes for pottery, particularly drinking cups with two arched handles known as *kantharoi,* became fashionable in Greece.[21] Amphorae, used for serving wine at the table, began to adopt Etruscan forms too, presumably to make them more appealing to buyers in Italy. One potter in particular, who was active in the mid-sixth century BCE, adopted these new forms, and we are lucky enough to know his name: Nikosthenes.[22] This individual

Black-figure neck amphora made in Orvieto showing a youth playing with a cat.

signed his name on 124 black-figure and nine red-figure vases that survive: a fragment of his total output.

Nikosthenes embraced Etruscan shapes – not only *kantharoi* and amphorae, but single-handled drinking cups (*kyathoi*) and cylindrical boxes (*pyxides*). However, the main output of his workshop were cups like ours from Chiusi – wide, flat-bottomed drinking vessels known as *kylikes* – a Greek shape.[23] They have flat handles and squat stems, making them tricky to use without spilling wine all down your front – a distinct advantage if you are trying to show off how sophisticated you are. From his decision to flatter Etruscan buyers, it seems clear that Nikosthenes was happy to invest in pleasing this market for his wares. That the Etruscan market sustained this large workshop is a testament to the value of this group of customers to Nikosthenes and his fellow craftspeople. Knowledge of Etruscan taste in pots must have been of great assistance to Nikosthenes, and questions about his own origins have begun to be asked.[24] Could it be possible that Nikosthenes was himself of Etruscan birth, a canny businessman who moved to Athens to profit from his homeland's taste for Attic vases in familiar shapes, and Etruscan-preferred imagery in Attic forms? We will never know, but the idea turns on its head Winckelmann's conception of Etruscan brutes lapping up Attic culture.

Our vase from Chiusi takes advantage of an invention that may be Nikosthenes' – the use of white pigment with incised black details. It is this technique that is used to create the elegant eyes that lie on each side of the human couple. Sadly, it is not from his workshop. The theme, a seated man and a standing woman, seems plain. What is it about this simple pot, and straightforward decoration, that made me choose it as the central object of this

Bucchero chalice with frieze of enthroned figures.

chapter? Certainly, there are more elaborate, more impressive vases from elsewhere in Etruria, complete with compelling images. This prosaic little scene, however, hints at a further adaptation of Greek vessels for the Etruscan market – namely, the transformation of imagery to better reflect Etruscan interests and Etruscan society. For Chiusi is famous for producing its own remarkable pottery decorated with the human form: glossy black bucchero wares, designed to catch the light and shimmer like bronze, many decorated with a frieze created from pressing a cylinder into the clay.[25] If you look at these pots, you can see, over and over again, a familiar scene.

One or sometimes two figures sit on stools. Before them stands a line of people. Some are clearly female, with deftly marked curves. Some are male, with long legs and short tunics. All these figures carry an object – a staff or spear, or what seems to be a length of cloth. Behind the enthroned figure(s) stands a strange creature – a winged

The same motif on another chalice.

woman. There is remarkable consistency in the production of these vessels, with this very specific scene repeated again and again. It was important for the people of Chiusi, and it was appropriate that this image be placed on a pot used for drinking. What the images seem to show is a formal gathering and presentation of gifts. Men and women together are present, and the act is blessed by the presence of a deity, who is depicted as literally the power behind the throne. Now, if we look at the images on the imported pot, we can see a clipped version of this scene. A woman holding a staff approaches a seated man. It is potentially a symbol of power, a gift that implies authority.[26] The two figures embody the central moment of the longer frieze, the exact point at which an obligation is created through giving. What we are seeing in this vase is potentially an awareness on the part of the painter of Chiusine taste. An inhabitant of this town, miles from a major trading port, found a shared meaning in this pot with the person who painted it across the sea.

This is not a relationship between inferior Etruscans and superior Greeks. Winckelmann's beliefs, and their influence, are incompatible with the idea of the Etruscan consumer dictating to an Attic artist. The valorization of Greek art has played a large part in removing the Etruscans from popular consciousness, yet how many of these supposed masterpieces would have been produced, let alone survived, without the influence and input of Etruscan owners and buyers? Ascribing value to a society based on what it produces is a problem, particularly when the value of that product is defined by something as arbitrary as beauty. The judgements we make about other people and their relationships with one another will always be more complex than they appear at first sight. The story of the Etruscan vases that became Greek reminds us that judging on first, and even second, impressions, is not a wise move. Making an assessment based on a hostile viewpoint is even more problematic.

This chapter has spiralled outwards from a little cup, and presented some of the most persistent tropes in Etruscan archaeology – the Etruscans as pirates, the Etruscans as barbarians. There is another viewpoint – the Etruscans as the saviours of classical art, the Etruscans as dictators of taste. Of course, it all depends on how you choose to interpret the evidence, the texts and the pots. Yet there are important issues wrapped up in this question of ancient taste. The same questions arise in relation to modern issues of globalization. Is Western culture dictating to other societies through the goods it demands and produces, or being subtly reshaped by its relationship with them? Are our preconceptions about the spread of ideas through objects, and the sharing of values, really accurate? This story of pots and of prejudice exposes the consequences of the unconscious bias that lies deep inside and that shapes our outlook on the world in a safe arena. The Etruscans don't care how we in the modern world portray them – they are safely dead. It is how we assess and respond to perceived difference and inequality among the living that really matters.

FIVE
Super Rich, Invisible Poor

All the Etruscan artefacts encountered so far in this book are associated with a particular group of privileged people. The individuals who owned, imported and commissioned these beautiful things were fortunate indeed. They had access to the best craftspeople, could wangle the most advantageous trade deals and could command the greatest respect after their death. These people are the most visible archaeologically; they were the rich and powerful, ensuring the survival of their possessions through their disposal of them. The problem is, by focusing in on these spectacular things, a great segment of Etruscan life disappears from view. The majority of Etruscan people would not have had access to such costly goods, and certainly would not have been able to invest so heavily in the commemoration of the dead. Their lives were certainly as complicated and fascinating as their richer contemporaries – they are just more difficult to trace.

Even the number of the less fortunate members of Etruscan society is a matter of speculation. Archaeologists have been seeking to estimate the population of Etruria for decades, but have mainly focused on the cities, using the size of each settlement as a guide.[1] It has been calculated that a small city like Chiusi may have been home to 5,000 people at its height, Tarquinia 20,000 and the largest cities of Veii and Cerveteri 32,000 and 25,000 respectively.[2] If we recognize that the total number of discovered tombs at Tarquinia is 6,000, and that these date from the ninth to the fourth centuries BCE, the disconnect between the number of burials and the total population size is startling. There are thousands of Etruscan people who simply vanish from the archaeological past. This is the major problem with focusing on artefacts from, and excavations of, tombs. You will only ever reach those who had both the resources and the inclination for formal burial.

By the end of the sixth century, more people were enjoying relative luxury in death – placement in a family tomb with a selection of grave goods. Simple, undecorated chamber tombs hint at the possibility of commemoration for the less wealthy, and the increased number of burials from this period suggest the growing proportion of Etruscan people who chose to formally dispose of their loved ones. Outside the cities and their associated burial places, the rural population, particularly the labourers, miners and craftspeople upon whose labour the wealth of Etruria was generated, are almost entirely invisible. There have been excavations of farmsteads, small sites in the countryside staffed largely by the have-nots, but the contrast between the scanty remains of these tiny settlements and the exuberant decoration of the tombs of the wealthy dead is vast.[3] One site, however, does seem to offer a little insight.

The site of Poggio Civitate has been an enigma in Etruscan archaeology since its discovery in the 1960s, but local people were

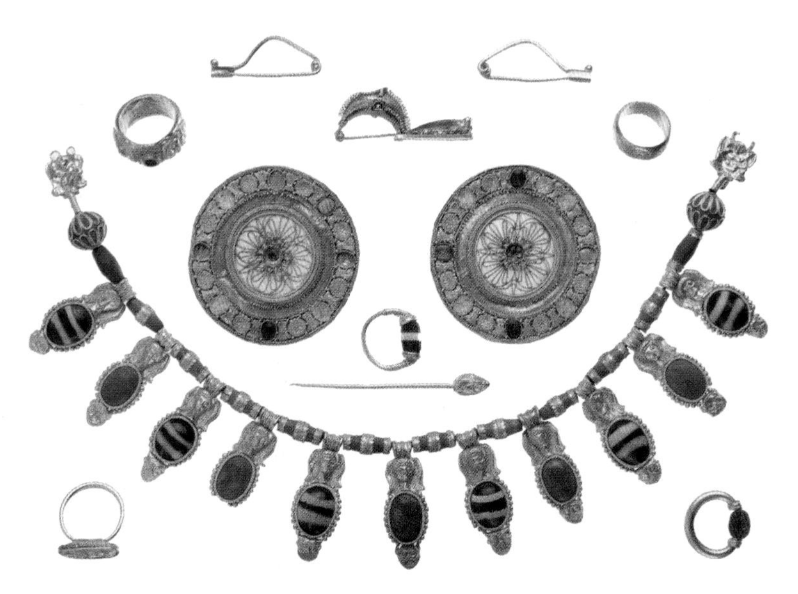

A remarkable set of jewellery thought to be from a tomb at Vulci.

already well aware of the site's existence. The first clues were stray finds, which had appeared during ploughing. Chief among these was an incredible bronze helmet.[4] When the famous Etruscan scholar Ranuccio Bianchi Bandinelli (1900–1975) stopped for lunch nearby, finds were rushed to his table.[5] Forty years later, he pointed a young American classicist, Kyle Meredith Phillips, to the location. The site he uncovered, Poggio Civitate, would dominate his life for the next thirty years, until his death in 1988. The site lies on the enigmatically named Piano del Tesoro, the plain of treasures. The name conjures up visions of gold and jewels, but if there were ever any finds of this value they are long gone. The treasure here is archaeological – a remarkable complex of buildings unlike any others in Etruria.

The earliest signs of occupation here are fragments of late Iron Age pottery, suggesting a settlement on this site from around the ninth century BCE onwards, although few traces of this first occupation survive.[6] However, in the early seventh century, three huge buildings were constructed on the plateau, beautifully decorated with elaborate terracotta friezes and topped with tiled roofs, a very recent innovation.[7] The three buildings have been interpreted as an elite residence, a workshop for producing the gorgeous craft items scattered across the site, and, tentatively, a religious space.[8] The residence was littered with expensive imported goods. It also contained items produced closer to home – just across the plateau, in what seems to have been a dedicated workshop space – an unusual survival from this period. This building was constructed with open sides, to let air in and let fumes and smoke out. It was topped by an expensive terracotta roof, providing shade and shelter from the rain – a serious investment in the work of the people toiling away below. The objects produced in this workshop were of high quality – carefully carved bone and ivory plaques used to decorate furniture, and the very best bucchero pottery, with its dark gleam reminiscent of the finest bronze.[9] Fingerprints of the workers survive in some of the items they produced, while their footprints were sealed forever in clay at the moment of the building's destruction.[10]

It was perhaps inevitable, with so many people working in close proximity, that accidents would happen. We cannot know about the smaller-scale incidents – broken bones, cuts and burns. One day, however, a craftsperson lost control of a fire. It seems to have been accidental, taking place while other workers were going about their daily tasks. All those within the workshop were forced to flee, some making their escape across a series of tiles laid out to dry, marking their presence for posterity. Ivory plaques were burnt, pots were smashed, their fragments refired by the flames. The fire spread across to the other buildings on the plateau, perhaps rushing through summer vegetation dried by the intense heat to perfect tinder. The single out-of-control workshop fire had become a raging inferno. The entire complex was destroyed. The inhabitants of Poggio Civitate were made of stern stuff, however, and rebuilding seems to have commenced quickly. The debris of the burned buildings was levelled and a new and even grander complex was up and running by the early sixth century.[11]

This new building was vast, the largest structure in the ancient Mediterranean at the time it was in use. It was built square, with a central courtyard, and topped with an even more elaborate terracotta tile roof. Each wing was 60 m in length, and a defensive wall added another 30 m to one side.[12] Looming over this enormous complex was a series of clay figurines, whose pose might be familiar from the previous chapter. Seated in formal chairs, male and female, they gazed down, their elaborate headgear casting a shadow on everyone below. This was the first building uncovered by Phillips in the 1960s, and its impact on the world of Etruscan archaeology was explosive. That such a building could exist in the middle of nowhere, far from any of the great cities described as the 'Etruscan League' by the Roman author Livy, was a serious shock.[13] The interpretations flowed in – it was the meeting place of the League on neutral territory, a supersized religious complex, or even a political and trading centre like an agora.[14]

None of these interpretations ever settled the question of the purpose of Poggio Civitate, particularly after the discovery of the earlier phases of the complex. The problem was that these ideas were so elaborate, so specific, that they felt far-fetched. They might match the ambitious scale of the complex, but did not reflect the actuality of life there, and certainly did not match the archaeological finds uncovered within it. The excavators felt convinced that the clear functions of the earlier buildings were incorporated within the central megastructure after the disastrous fire. The workers were probably moved to a so far undiscovered area, possibly under stricter controls and probably to prevent future accidents engulfing the new central complex. By contrast, the ritual building became literally part of the fabric of the residence, tied entirely to the family living within, and cementing their privileged connection with the divine. These people were part of the elite social networks that stretched for hundreds of miles, binding the rich and powerful together through shared interests and values. The fabulous artefacts laid to rest with the dead, and the elaborate tombs of the southern coastal cities, were made and designed for this peer group.

Their enviable lifestyle is illustrated by some of the finds from the sixth-century building, and some of its most meaningful moments are recorded in the friezes which once decorated it. The pottery is particularly telling, providing evidence for the consumption of wine on a grand scale.[15] The animal bones from the site include a large proportion of pigs, animals that are solely raised for the table. Wild animals, too, appear, suggesting hunting provided high-status additions to the diet of Poggio Civitate's high society.[16] Scenes of dogs hunting hares decorate parts of the building, while the tusks of dangerous wild boars attest to their hunting and consumption on a large scale. The kind of event that these pots would have been used at, and these animals served at, is depicted on one

Architectural terracotta relief from Poggio Civitate, a perplexing site from Central Etruria.

Elaborate bucchero banqueting set with plates.

form of the four types of decorative terracotta frieze plaques, showing diners on elaborate couches. Men and women feast together. To be able to command enough resources to provide this kind of hospitality is a statement of wealth and confidence. Providing food and drink at this level illustrates the family's control of territory and labour, but is also a testament to the fertility of their lands and productivity of their people. The suggestion is that you cannot enjoy such bounty without divine favour, so the representation of this activity makes a series of important points, all of which return to the central issue – the superiority of Poggio Civitate's owners to the ordinary people around them.[17]

The carved bone plaques which once decorated furniture are another marker of extreme wealth. To have the very chair you sit on made beautiful suggests a dedication to beauty, as well as to functionality. Each individual plaque would have taken a worker hours to produce, with etchings on a tiny scale. The number of such plaques required to make up a single piece of furniture can be seen on a chair from Verucchio, preserved by waterlogged soil conditions.[18] The total time taken to produce such a masterpiece is awe-inspiring, and the inhabitants of the Poggio Civitate complex appear to have had a cohort of skilled workers at their service. The clay figures on the roofs, seated on their elaborate chairs, are no doubt intended to be posing on such richly decorated pieces of furniture. The scene is repeated again in another of the sequence of frieze plaques, showing enthroned male and female figures sitting in state on the same cross-legged stools familiar from the Chiusi vase.

Among the animal bones from the complex are the remains of one of the most expensive animals of the ancient world – the horse. The time it takes to break a horse or pony to ride and drive, the investment of skill and effort in the process, in addition to acquiring the beast in the first place, made these animals the equivalent of a luxury car. Far more than a mode of transport, the possession and successful control of a large equine made a statement about its owner. Fast horses were the equivalent of the Ferraris that cruise the autostrada in the present day. It is this kind of animal that is represented in the Poggio Civitate frieze plaques.[19] This shows a series of riders in a madcap bareback race. The horses depicted are in full flight, with the riders leaning forward to urge

The Monteleone chariot – luxury transport for the afterlife of the Etruscan super rich, 6th century, bronze and ivory.

Highly elaborate Villanovan horse bit: no less a status symbol than the horse itself.

them on. The context of the race is not clear; that it is a race at all and not a procession is implied by the presence of a prize – an enormous pot, a *krater*. Whatever the occasion, owning three very valuable animals, being skilled enough to ride them at high speed and being confident enough to risk their loss (a broken limb would mean the death of an animal) smacks of extreme wealth.

The final frieze plaque scene also features expensive horses. This time they are busy pulling a two-wheeled cart. A couple sit towards the front of the vehicle, which is definitely a cart, not a chariot.[20] One of the figures holds an elaborate staff – a composition which should sound familiar by now. Behind the cart is a procession of people. They seem to be carrying a selection of goods – semi-circular objects which look like fans, and square-shaped boxes. Once again, the horses demonstrate the wealth and reach of the central couple, underlined by their attendants who follow behind on foot. This image has been interpreted as a wedding procession – the arrival of the bride into a new family, bringing her possessions and household with her.[21] Whether this specific context is an accurate reflection of what is going on here is perhaps not important. What is clear is that a display of serious wealth is taking place. Whatever this event was, it was so impressive it literally became iconic.

People all over the world love to tell stories about the places they live in. The ability of humans to mythologize even the most mundane locations, to elevate simple events to great importance, allows us to remake the world in our own image. In a place as extraordinary as Poggio Civitate, these stories are retold in the very fabric of the building. The impression of the entire complex to a visitor must have been phenomenal. Everywhere you looked, from the moment of arrival, you would see evidence of the wealth and power of your hosts. Their ancestors, glaring down from the roof, were only the first sight of a building dedicated to familial propaganda. The people living here could overcome disaster within a generation. Rebuilt from the ashes, the new complex speaks of thousands of hours of labour, while its decorative details are a statement that its owners shared in the elite passions of hunting and racing, and valued occasions that called for processions and audiences. The stories that this family told about themselves were built into the walls of their home, reaffirming their shared sense of superiority every time they caught a glimpse of them.

The stories of the labourers and craftspeople did not enjoy the same privilege. The question of what happened to *these* people, how they lived their lives, has remained an unanswered question for the excavators of Poggio Civitate. Surely, such an enormous complex could not have existed unsupported. But if so, where did these workers live? They presumably did not share the seventh-century residence, and move in to the grand complex of the sixth-century reconstruction. There is no sign of buildings akin to later Roman slave quarters. In the mid-2000s, excavations did reveal a settlement at the village of Vescovado di Murlo, about 3 km away from Poggio Civitate, but these remains of kilns and houses were from far later than their hilltop neighbour.[22] Could small satellite settlements at this kind of distance have supplied the labour required to keep Poggio Civitate going? Probably not. Then where were the support staff, and how could the excavators discover them?

In 2012 excavations began on both sides of a medieval road which snakes across the site. On the southern side, erosion had resulted in a series of deposits from the Etruscan period. On the north side, however, there were intriguing signs of small-scale buildings and industrial activity. Vast quantities of slag and debris from metalworking appeared. Lines of large rocks, carefully uncovered by the team, began to look like the outlines of walls. In 2013 the excavators exposed more of this area. Assisted by aerial photography, it became clear that they had found a series of small buildings, probably houses. They were built in two phases, transforming from oblong- to rectangular-shaped dwellings. The patterns of finds, with rubbish including animal bones, broken coarse ware pottery and terracotta tile fragments outside of the line of each structure's wall, suggested their use as dwellings, kept clean inside with the rubbish dumped outside. These buildings were also, as the first discoveries in this area suggested, being used for industrial purposes. It seems certain that bronze was being made here, and broken fragments of carved bone suggest that these items too were being produced. The workers of Poggio Civitate were visible at last.[23]

Excavation is ongoing in this area as the team try to establish the extent of this supporting settlement. The current interpretation is that the two phases of building here mirror that on the adjacent plateau, although there is no sign of the telltale layer of burnt debris that would suggest the fire spread here. There is a deliberately blocked-up well nearby, so you could expect that more dwellings might be found between this water source, the 2013 discoveries and the major complex on Piano del Tesoro. These buildings provide a tantalizing glimpse into the lives of the people who made Poggio Civitate work. At least some of them were living in stone-built houses, sharing in the architectural techniques used in the construction of the massive complex of their wealthy neighbours. They were skilled craftspeople (something already obvious from the quality of locally produced goods already found in and around the plateau) who were allowed or encouraged to bring their work home with them. They had access to a range of goods and foods that, while not as impressive as those enjoyed by the occupants of the major buildings, do not suggest a high degree of want or scarcity. However, there is no question of equality here. Fragments of high-quality goods are most likely broken cast-offs, recycled and scavenged. The structures are minute in comparison with the vast extent of the neighbouring complex. There was a stark difference between the quality of life of these people and those living just metres away.

The excavations of 2012 and 2013 brought another, more macabre, discovery. It is a truism that a society can be judged by how it treats the most vulnerable. These recent discoveries have shown that some of the weakest, smallest members of the community at Poggio Civitate were not being treated well.[24] Since the 1960s, a large archive of skeletal remains from all over the site had been built up and stored for future analysis. Each context was meticulously recorded so that the collection remained coherently linked to the archaeology on and under the ground. In 2012, examination of this huge archaeological resource began. Mixed in with the animal bones, from the very same contexts, were some tiny, fragile pieces that were unmistakably human on expert inspection. At first, it seemed a freak event, perhaps caused by erosion. The infant remains had come from an area of the site excavated years ago; could their presence be a quirk of collection, or a missed burial?

Very quickly, it became clear that this was not an exceptional incident. More infant remains began to emerge from the clear plastic sacks of animal bones. Then a fragment was found *in situ* in one of the areas under active excavation.[25] There was no question of a burial having been missed. This was part of the remains of a child, discarded along with industrial waste and animal bone in what was undeniably the poorer part of the site. It was a reminder that behind the grand architecture and beautiful craftsmanship lay a dark reality of hardship and suffering. Infant mortality has been estimated at thirty deaths per one hundred pregnancies during the later Roman period – and this rate could apply to the Etruscan period too.[26] The causes of death for a young baby in a world without vaccinations and with poor perinatal hygiene are myriad. Recent analysis of an Athenian infant burial site, inside an abandoned well, suggests that the majority of its tiny occupants died of meningitis caused by infection after the cutting of the umbilical cord.[27] With no sterile instruments, a dirty bronze blade could introduce bacteria into a vulnerable little immune system effortlessly, with fatal results.

Faced with the knowledge that many pregnancies would end with no living baby, it is possible that the inhabitants of Poggio Civitate made a decision not to commemorate or value these inevitable losses. A tragic waste, an inevitable consequence, a dangerous risk – welcoming a new life into the world must have been fraught with anxiety and fear. It may be that Etruscan social practices deliberately denied the right of an infant to life, until it had survived the first pitfalls of babyhood.[28] The idea of personhood – that some individuals do not count as people – is important here. If so many babies died so young, their commemoration would have been a sinkhole of time and energy. Any grief of the parents themselves is made invisible to modern eyes by the burial ritual deemed appropriate for the bodies: their disposal alongside other forms of waste. The relationships these babies left behind, and the physical and mental pain of their parents, are impossible to reconstruct. What is clear, however, is that at least symbolically these infants were not valued by the society into which they were born. These smallest, weakest, most vulnerable members of the Poggio Civitate community seem to have suffered in life and been deliberately forgotten in death. Their scattered remains are a stark contrast to the careful and deliberate burials of the rich and powerful on the neighbouring hill of Poggio Aguzzo.

The contrast between rich and poor at Poggio Civitate is also echoed in the modern world's extreme variation in economic wealth. The redistribution of wealth by the very rich through charitable funds was probably not a feature of Etruscan life – but the spending of vast sums on self-promotion and luxury living is a constant theme in human enjoyment of wealth. The enormous complex at Poggio Civitate is akin to the super villas of the Tuscan countryside, beginning with those of Roman landowners, continuing with medieval aristocrats including the Medici, and ending with those of footballers and millionaires. Normal life continues outside, with workers in small homes going about their daily business as the super-rich luxuriate in their tabloid inches and swimming pools. Just as in the archaeological record at Poggio

Elaborate gold earrings from the 6th century.

Civitate, the culture of the very rich continues to dominate our desires and awareness, while the lives of the poor leave behind only ephemeral traces, ignored in favour of glitz and glamour.

The tale of Poggio Civitate could be interpreted in this left-wing fashion – its end certainly plays to a socialist fairy tale. The reconstructed complex would be brutally destroyed in a deliberate act of violence. The largest Etruscan building known would not survive to universal acclaim like its Greek counterparts. Instead, it was torn down, the architectural terracotta decorations smashed and buried in pits. Anything valuable was presumably seized and carried off; very little metalwork or imported ceramics survive from this phase. The site's water sources were blocked up with debris, ensuring that no one would ever be able to live there again. Excavations in 2015 have even hinted at the violent nature of the destruction, with human remains uncovered in association with one particular well.[29] There is no hint of what happened to spark this devastation. The temptation is to suggest that the workers of Poggio Civitate might have risen up against the elite family who controlled their lives – perhaps in response to their perceived failure in controlling the fertility of the land. This is pure speculation, playing to a proletarian dream; it could be that the site was the victim of another city's rage.

Whoever they were, the destroyers of the site did their work well; it would remain unoccupied for thousands of years, with only itinerant shepherds and wild boar hunters disturbing the peace of the site. The land has been owned by the great Hospital of Santa Maria in Siena for the past thousand years or so – it remains covered in scrub forest, with the lines of stones marking the homes of rich and poor covered in wild grasses. When the archaeologists leave, the contrast between the luxuriant surroundings of the site's leading family and the cramped quarters of its workers vanishes once again beneath backfilled soil and dead leaves. But the questions the site prompts over the reality and consequences of inequality in Etruscan society are not so easy to erase.

Statuette of a young woman, late 6th century, probably made in Chiusi or Vulci.

SIX

To Be a Woman

Inequality is an uncomfortable subject – in archaeology and in society today. Different groups are marked out for discrimination or promotion on the basis of their bodies and/or their situation in life. The colour of a person's skin, or their ethnic origin, or their socio-economic status, may influence their treatment in the past and in the present. A further distinction is often made based on a person's biological sex – defined here as the presence or absence of particular physical equipment. The existence of a penis or vagina at birth begins a process of socialization. The raw material of a baby grows and shifts, through physical, mental and social influences, to become a gendered adult. In a liberal Euro-American worldview, we can acknowledge that the gender of adults is non-binary. That is, there is no simple equation of man does not equal woman. Trans- and other gendered people are increasingly (and thankfully) accepted. Yet the initial presence or absence of particular kinds of bodily parts continues to be a major influence on any person's life – they still define our senses of self, whether through acceptance or resentment.

The Etruscan world also divided people by their bodies. Largely, male and female bodies are distinguished from one another – by clothing, by the shape of the body, and by skin colour in the case of tomb paintings.[1] An Etruscan person might not have had the same conception of what a man or woman is, nor the relationship between biological sex and social gender. While we can hint at exceptional individuals, or behaviours which do not correspond to modern gender roles, bodily difference does seem to have mattered for the Etruscans. We might suggest that religious figures could be considered a third gender, or argue for the recognition of individuals with trans-type experiences.[2] But it is the perceived difference between male and female lives, and the representation of the behaviour of Etruscan women, that lies at the heart of this chapter. In this instance, the lack of surviving texts written by Etruscan authors is a positive leveller; no truly authentic portrait of Etruscan women's experiences survives at all, regardless of the gender of its author.

In the archaeological record, however, women's bodies and possessions doggedly survive to tell their stories. At least, they do if we have the ability to listen. Archaeologists have a bad track record in the interpretation of women's lives; witness the endless enthusiasm for stereotypes of male innovation, action and power – and female passivity.[3] Examples are strewn across the archaeological world: the steady refusal to acknowledge any female in the past as capable of possessing personal power denied in the present. Even when a woman is buried with incredibly rich grave goods, they are relegated to the position of chattels – objects that state her worth to a male owner, be he father, husband or brother.[4] Women are wives and daughters, mothers and sisters – not traders, owners, makers. Incredible interpretations are put forward to explain exceptional women; they can be elevated through association with religion, or linked to legends of women warriors. In recent years feminist archaeologists have been fighting these prejudices and reclaiming the archaeological story of women's lives in the past – but they have yet to be taken seriously beyond their own spheres of influence.

As feminist archaeology was beginning to gain some traction, large cemeteries of cremation burials were used to develop one of the first studies of women's lives in Etruria, mapping the connections between particular grave goods and the probable genders of their owners.[5] The results were conclusive, the majority of male burials contained weapons, while the majority of female burials incorporated equipment for spinning and weaving. They seemed to be a relatively mutually exclusive form of grave goods – either weaving kits or weapons. Yet this initial research on an

Alabaster perfume vessel in the form of a woman.

early period could already identify exceptions – burials with both types of object, or neither. Other materials found in graves confused the picture even further; is a burial with a razor and jewellery automatically male, or automatically female, according to this categorization system? Assumptions about gender based on artefacts are deeply problematic. Without DNA analysis of the cremated remains, it is a complex and uncertain task to even check the initial assumption that women were weavers and men were warriors – and this type of analysis has yet to take place.

The conclusions of this analysis of the gender of occupants of biconical urns holds true for later Etruscan burials too. Unfortunately, different people have different ideas of what those conclusions might be. Archaeologists influenced by feminist thought might think that the study demonstrated the existence of individuals who crossed gender boundaries. A more traditional approach, based on assumptions about male and female labour, would ignore these nuances and go with the broad sweep of the data. Both camps would choose the interpretation that suits their prejudices. However, for later burials, there is an opportunity missing from the urn cemeteries. In rare cases, where tombs have not been robbed out entirely, or excavated by antiquarians with the sale of Attic pots on their minds, a body may survive. While objects can tell one version of a story, the body tells another – and the presence of a skeleton largely removes the need for DNA analysis to identify the biological sex of the long dead person.

So, when an untouched tomb was uncovered in Tarquinia in the autumn of 2013, and a skeleton found inside, a rare opportunity arose. Local, national and international media gathered as the excavators presented their findings. The tomb contained, in addition to the skeleton laid out on one of its benches, a cremation burial inside a decorated urn. Hanging on the wall was a well-preserved perfume vessel, which gave the sepulchre its name – the Tomb of the Hanging Aryballos. This remarkable tomb is the central object for this chapter, and it is certainly one of the most important discoveries in twenty-first-century Etruscan archaeology. There were other pots scattered around the entrance to the tomb – typical banqueting sets. A grater was included, used to add cheese to wine, as described by Homer. Inside the tomb, lying on the body itself, was a spear. Also laid on the body were a bronze box, a bronze basin and a decorated pot filled with brooches known as fibulae. The team who excavated this tomb, from the University of Turin, put together the spear with the rich trappings and came up with their initial interpretation: the burial was that of a male of high status. The assembled media quickly transformed the original statement; the tomb was now that of a warrior prince.[6] The print and online media lapped up the story – for a short time, the forgotten Etruscans were big news. In the meantime, the archaeologists carefully concluded their work. The initial analysis of the pots confirmed a date of the seventh century BCE. The analysis continued; the metal finds were passed on to conservators, while an osteoarchaeologist, a specialist in human bone, took charge of the skeleton. It was at this point that the runaway narrative of the warrior prince was proved to be incorrect.[7] The skeletal remains were demonstrably female.

A conundrum, then. Who was this woman, to be buried with such remarkable grave goods? Later discussions of the tomb by the excavation team have hinted at the spear being symbolic – perhaps of union between the woman and the cremated individual, a male. This rather vague interpretation reflects the strength of patriarchal views in archaeology; better to appeal to an unknown ritual than to acknowledge the potential of women's power in the past. In later publications, the woman was downgraded to a 'seamstress', with all the overtones of servitude and domesticity that term provides.[8] The combination of sewing kit and weapons, already present in earlier burials at Tarquinia, could be indicative of a way of life that incorporated both skill with cloth and a relationship with weapons. Symbolic or not, the presence of the spear suggests an affinity with aggression, control, violence. These are the associations of weapons, whether used directly by this woman or on her behalf. Was there room for a powerful woman like this in Etruscan society?

The legend of Etruscan women would suggest so. Indeed, the reputation of Etruscan women was so strong that their independence is one of the few features of Etruscan society that remains widely known – it is a key part of the Etruscan myth. Women are regularly represented in Etruscan imagery, enthroned alongside men in images on ceramics and decorative terracottas. Female faces and bodies feature in the friezes that decorated great Etruscan buildings. In tomb paintings, women are shown dining with men, equally gorgeously attired, seated on the same couches. These scenes are made eternal in sarcophagi and cinerary urns, on which women recline with their partners or alone.[9] They share the same food, the same access to alcohol, the same luxuries as their men, and seem to have enjoyed equal respect as ancestors too. Inscriptions from tombs name their occupants, connecting them not only with their father, but with their mother and her family as well, recognizing the importance of the female line of descent.[10] Goddesses, too, are

Frescoes of the Tomb of the Leopards, Tarquinia.

represented again and again, enshrining women's bodies with divine power, the addition of wings and presence of wild beasts demonstrating their control over the natural and supernatural worlds.

These are all images of wealthy or even divine women, who perhaps might be expected to enjoy a different experience. Checking Etruscan privilege, however, it seems that a culture of relative respect for women existed at other levels of society too. In presentation scenes in which gifts are given to presumed rulers, the people who hand over their produce are both male and female. The crafts that wealthy women practised with expensive bronze tools were also undertaken using more basic instruments of rough clay and carved bone. These tools, for weaving and spinning, were often decorated or marked with symbols, suggesting personal ownership of the objects that create wealth. These women of a lower social status are more difficult to trace archaeologically, as are their relationships with the men around them, but the signs are there. If a woman owned her own weaving equipment and marked it with her personal symbol, it could follow that the goods she produced were hers to use as she desired. The tools cannot tell us – but if rich women are acknowledged in funerary inscriptions, it is possible that poor women could have been acknowledged too.

Acknowledgement does not equal equality, however. The term relative is important here. Compared with other cultures in the ancient Mediterranean, Etruscan women may have enjoyed a more privileged experience to their counterparts elsewhere.[11] In Athens, respectable women would rarely leave their personal quarters within the family home, excluded even from the *andron*, the male dining space. Their only escape would be for religious festivals, or funerals, and possible visits to female friends. The existence of a different kind of woman – whether a ferocious Amazon or independent Etruscan – needed to be dismissed as barbarism to protect the status quo. Later, Roman women, while having a greater degree of freedom, were not to be encouraged by the example of Etruscan female behaviour.[12] Roman authors share the discomfort of their

Female antefix, probably from an Etruscan temple at Cerveteri.

Greek fellows when discussing the behaviour of Etruscan women – and it is their work that really underlies the survival of the concept of independent women in Etruria. Indeed, Livy places Etruscan women at the heart of the foundation of the Roman Republic.

While dating foundation myths is a problematic pastime, the supposed events of this story took place around the last decade of the sixth century BCE. A Roman nobleman, Tarquinius Collatinus, dines with the son of the then Etruscan ruler of his city, Sextus Tarquinius. The two men, after an evening of drinking, argue over whose wife is more virtuous. Heading first to the king's household they discover that his Etruscan wife has been enjoying herself too – in Livy's words, has been 'banqueting with friends'.[13] By contrast, over at Tarquinius Collatinus' mansion, the virtuous Lucretia is angelically 'working at her wool by lamplight'. Lucretia's behaviour is an example for any good Roman matron – she is dedicated to womanly crafts, not to the pleasures of the dinner table and wine jug. It doesn't do her any good though. Her perfection inspires the lust of the wicked Sextus Tarquinius; days later, he returns to Lucretia's home and rapes her. After naming him to her husband, father and two of their trusted friends, Lucretia commits suicide. Her husband and father join together, and run the dissolute ruling family of Sextus Tarquinius out of town. The Etruscan women of the house of Tarquinius are responsible, indirectly, for the downfall of their men; their dedication to a party lifestyle exemplifies the rotten morality of their wider family. When women behave against the strict Roman moral code Livy idolized, society is damaged irreparably, and death, defeat and exile will undoubtedly follow.[14]

The nameless Etruscan women of the tale of Lucretia seem to have lost their places in Rome through innocent enjoyment, sharing a banquet together. However, the mother and grandmother of Sextus Tarquinius, Tullia and Tanaquil, were not only part of what Livy describes as a lascivious household – they were expert politicians, who would not hesitate to further their familial power.[15] According to legend, Tanaquil was a high-born daughter of the city of Tarquinia, married to the son of a migrant, a Greek from Corinth named Demaratus. She knew that his birth excluded her husband, who bore the ingratiating name Tarquinius, from power in her native city, so demanded they move to Rome. The couple wormed their way into the confidence of the then ruler of the city, and grabbed power on his death. The figure of Tanaquil, as depicted by Livy, Pliny the Elder and Cassius Dio, brings together a number of stereotypes of Etruscan women.[16] She is described as a prophetess, a woman who could read omens and interpret dreams. When her husband's hat was stolen by an eagle, then politely returned to him, Tanaquil instantly recognized this strange event as a sign from the gods. Later, after a vision, Tanaquil would acknowledge the royal potential of her foster-son Servius Tullius. While the young man slept, his head appeared engulfed in flames, which disappeared when he awoke. Tanaquil would interpret this visitation as a symbol of divine favour. More prosaically, Tanaquil is also described as an excellent worker of wool. She emerges relatively unscathed from Roman writings, unusually for an Etruscan woman. Looking back at her story, a defining feature is the consistent application of her talents (whether in political manipulation, reading omens or spinning) in the service of her husband. Tanaquil's powers are harnessed by a male benefactor, and made safe in the critical eyes of later male writers.

Her daughter-in-law, Tullia, preferred to scheme on her own behalf, plotting against the men in her life. As a result, she emerges alongside her son as one of the great villains of Roman literature. Tullia was the daughter of Servius Tullius, Tanaquil's foster-son and by now king of Rome. In a double wedding designed to bring the two families even closer together, Tullia and her older sister were married to Tanaquil's two sons. Tullia was married to the more relaxed of the two, Arruns, while her peace-loving sister was shackled to the ambitious Lucius. Inevitably, Tullia and her brother-in-law became deeply attracted to one another, and conspired to murder their respective spouses. Married at last, the evil pair plotted to grab the throne for themselves. It was on Tullia's orders that Lucius, accompanied by a band of thugs, stormed the seat of government, Senate House. As dictated by his wife, Lucius threw his father-in-law out of the window. Landing in the filth of the gutter, he was murdered by assassins paid by Tullia. The lady herself added the final indignity. Dressed to kill in her luxurious carriage, she drove down to the Senate House. Whipping up her horses, she drove directly over the body of her father.

Tullia's actions put her in a special category of vicious womanhood. The killing of a close relation was one of the most heinous crimes dealt with by Roman justice; Livy calls Tullia's behaviour 'a foul and unnatural crime'. The punishment, under the later law codes, was to be bound in a leather sack with a selection of animals. The leather sack would then be flung, with its occupants, into a river or lake. The leather of the bag would prolong the process, ensuring that slow suffocation, or painful injuries from animal bites, would finish off the criminal. Yet Tullia escapes; her husband does become king, she is rewarded, albeit temporarily, for her foul behaviour. Contrary to these appearances, Livy is clear that a bad end was unavoidable for this harridan. He states that Tullia's actions offended the gods, who caused the downfall of her family. In their flight from Rome, Tullia is marked by the people as responsible – Livy portrays her as bombarded with abuse by the men and women of the city, 'invoking her father's avenging spirit'.[17]

These Etruscan women, as portrayed by Livy, are exceptional characters. Together with the unnamed daughters-in-law of the house of Tarquinius, this portrait of a royal family in crisis provides a Roman view on Etruscan women. Crucial observations seep through the hyperbole, however. Tullia and Tanaquil alike see the possession of authority as their absolute right. In both cases, it is through the actions of these women that men rule: the promotion of Servius Tullius by Tanaquil to the detriment of her own sons, and his murder by Tullia to secure the throne for her husband. Reading the will of the gods, working with cloth and the bearing of children are all activities which allow women to gain status for themselves. Claiming connection with the divine, producing high-quality goods for sale and the magical process of pregnancy and birth – these are all features of the Tarquinii wives as described by Livy that we might claim for other Etruscan women. Putting them together with the banquets enjoyed by their nameless relations, the account suggests that Etruscan women were able to not only earn wealth and power, but enjoy its more pleasurable consequences for themselves. The point that Livy's account makes is that such a strong position for women can only end in trouble: unnatural murder, alienation from the gods and exile and death.

With such compelling tales of Etruscan women in historical sources, it's no surprise that later accounts repeat their stories. Boccaccio (1313–1375) includes Tanaquil in his collection of biographies of famous women, *De mulieribus claris,* usually translated as 'On Famous Women'.[18] Tanaquil is the Etruscan representative, albeit under her adopted Roman name of Gaia Cyrilla. Boccaccio's work enshrines the stereotype of independence for Etruscan women in literature. His piece was composed for the sister of a high-ranking Neapolitan dignitary, serving the powerful and scandalous Queen Joanna of Naples. The queen herself stood trial for the murder of her husband, strangled by jealous nobles with his pregnant wife in the next room.[19] Unlike Tullia, however, Joanna of Naples was acquitted of involvement in her husband's murder, and would go on to be the final woman celebrated in Boccaccio's account. The tales of these Etruscan women in an early Renaissance court, alongside more traditional role models, must have provided not only entertainment but inspiration for Joanna and her ladies. Boccaccio's depiction also influenced the course of English literary history: this work was the direct inspiration for Chaucer's *Legend of Good Women* (*c.* 1387). While Tanaquil herself does not appear in this later work, the Roman Lucretia does. It is her story that carries the legend of Etruscan female misbehaviour forward into English texts. Tanaquil's more positive qualities are left behind in Latin.

What Chaucer began, another literary giant continued two centuries later. Shakespeare's epic poem, *The Rape of Lucrece* (1594), features these same Etruscan women. The verse itself deals with Sextus Tarquinius' encounter with Lucretia and her tragic final meeting with her husband. However, in the prologue given by Shakespeare to contextualize his poem, the great man gives Etruscan women a fraction of his attention: 'The other ladies were all found dancing and revelling, or in several disports.' This brief description goes even further than Livy in representing the women of the Tarquinii as loose-living creatures. The 'several disports' has an implication beyond its official definition of unrestrained enjoyment.

Shakespeare is hinting that the contrast between the Etruscan women and his version of Lucretia is sexual. She is later described as 'Lucrece the chaste', and it is implied that Sextus Tarquinius' lust is inspired precisely by the novelty of her chastity: 'Haply that name of "chaste" unhappily set / This bateless edge on his keen appetite.' (Act I. 2).

Etruscan women have also been seen as an influence on *Macbeth*, and the character of Lady Macbeth herself.[20] Shakespeare is thought to have read a Kentish writer, William Painter (1540?–1594), who adapted Livy's pen portraits of Tullia and Tanaquil into his work *Two Roman Queenes* (1575). Lines given by Painter to Tullia are adapted by Shakespeare for Lady Macbeth, and the parallel in their stories is obvious: their shared desire for power, their careful manipulation of a husband, their willingness to murder. While the two women are described as Romans by Painter, with Shakespeare's knowledge of Etruscan female behaviour evident in *The Rape of Lucrece*, it is likely that he recognized the relationship between these infamous Etruscan women and his darkest villainess. Later in the seventeenth century, Tullia would be used as a propaganda figure, denigrating Mary II after her occupation of the English throne and exile of her father, James II. The Etruscan woman was firmly established in the early-modern consciousness as a figure of political intrigue and loose morals.

The problem with the textual sources is that they feature a very small group of Etruscan women in extraordinary circumstances. They serve a narrative purpose – for Livy as much as for Shakespeare. Yes, there are some tiny fragments of truth that might be gleaned from these accounts: the value of women's labour, their relationship with the divine, their ability to organize and share evening entertainments together. Yet they can also be discarded as unreliable, with male-centred interpretations of Etruscan archaeology well able to ignore any historical descriptions of women's power beyond the household. On the other hand, in the context of feminist rewriting of history, it is possible to put together the representations of Etruscan women in the company of men, enjoying the same activities, and their similar treatment in death, to conclude that Etruria was an ancient feminist utopia. Yet this would be utterly simplistic – as erroneous as the misogynistic version. Terms used throughout this chapter – equality, independence – are deeply specific to our own culture. What does it truly mean for a woman to be equal? Equal pay for equal work? We will never know what Etruscan women were paid for their cloth production, and what their male equivalents earned. Equal rights to children and respect in the family? A name on a tomb does not equal a society where mothers are given the same respect and responsibility as fathers. Equal opportunities? Sharing a banqueting couch with a male partner does not guarantee protection from that partner, and the right to refuse them after dinner.

We will never know the exact nature of women's lives in Etruscan Italy. Yet their appearances, both in archaeological materials and in texts, continue to expose the inadequacies in our modern, supposedly egalitarian society. The discovery of the Tomb of the Hanging Aryballos was a remarkable moment for Etruscan archaeology. It was an opportunity for inventiveness, for excitement. Instead, traditional, male-dominated views came to overshadow the discussion. The woman whose bones had triggered all the fuss in the first place was sidelined. Expectations for women's lives in the past remain secured to women's experiences in the present. The story of the woman of the Hanging Aryballos could be one of the most fascinating ever imagined – her connection to the spearhead and the expensive perfume vessel, her relationship with her tomb-mate. Instead, she is just another dull seamstress buried with a warrior. How many modern women continue to be defined by restricting stereotypes, their horizons carefully trimmed to a sexist definition of mother, worker, thinker, politican? Gendered assumptions dog women in the present just as they conceal the experiences of women in the past.

The Etruscan women as portrayed by Livy, Boccaccio and Shakespeare have an even darker connection to the modern world. The rape of Lucretia is clearly an episode of extreme misogyny – perpetrated by the supposedly woman-friendly Etruscans. However, it is the conduct of their own women that is blamed for the violent attack on an innocent. Women are responsible for the abuse of other women: it is their foul behaviour, their lack of morality, which leads to the violation and murder of someone utterly blameless. The same logic prevails in the twenty-first century, through the rationale of street harassment, sexual abuse and the recent phenomenon of revenge porn. Any woman who dares to enjoy herself, and particularly any woman who might take pleasure in sexual play, is not only a valid target herself, but is responsible for the mistreatment of others. She must be punished through public shaming – the promotion of a sex tape, the distribution of her private photographs on the Internet, the screaming headlines in the tabloid press. The modern 'Etruscan' woman, partying the night away, is still not to be pitied if on the way home she is attacked. Victim blaming remains a deep issue in the reporting of sexual crime, and can have a vicious impact on the psyche of the target of an attack.

The dominance of the story of Etruscan women as unusually independent continues to provoke. However, it is only by breaking this stereotype down into the individual experiences of different Etruscan women from all levels of society that we can hope to understand their position within society and the joys and sorrows of their lives. It is the only way that remarkable remains like those in the Tomb of the Hanging Aryballos can be fully understood. It is also the only way to move on from Livy and his heirs, exposing the variety of Etruscan women's lives. This same idea has a chance of changing the present, too. By cataloguing women's experiences of abuse, they are empowered. Providing evidence proves the continued existence of these ancient problems. Perhaps the stereotype of the independent Etruscan woman can, in this manner, become real.

SEVEN

Safe as Houses

So far, this book has largely followed a familiar yet problematic pattern in Etruscan archaeology. It is an issue defined by the title of one of the most famous studies of Etruscan culture, a nickname that has stuck fast: 'The Buried People'.[1] Spectacular Etruscan tombs, their wonderful contents and bright paintings, have made archaeologists rabbits in the headlights, blinded by the glories of death.[2] The broader detritus of life – the broken bits and pieces, the discarded rubbish – is masked behind this glamorous facade. These items are not to be found in burials, but in back-streets. The excavations at Poggio Civitate have revealed a huge amount of new information, as described earlier, but this is far from a 'normal' Etruscan town. Field surveys and digs that have uncovered ancient farmsteads and homesteads, too, are beginning to expose the intricacies of life in the Etruscan countryside. However, the down and dirty reality of many Etruscan lives lies hidden beneath modern settlements. The great cities of Etruria were ideally located, and remained occupied for centuries, even into the present day.

Smaller, more isolated towns are the places to turn to to explore the remains of the Etruscans at home. The site at the centre of this chapter lies to the north of the cities discussed so far. It follows the unwritten law of Etruscan real estate, in that its location is idyllically beautiful. The ancient city of Marzabotto is tucked on a spur above the River Reno. The valley is steep sided – these are not the rolling hills of Tuscan postcards. The air is different here, even in the heat of summer. The hazy, golden fields of the south are gone, and the forest is thicker, darker. In winter, the snows, which further south are a nuisance, are a menace. On this site lies a rare survivor, one of the best-preserved Etruscan centres still in existence. Marzabotto is a short drive from Bologna, another Etruscan city, now completely hidden by modern sprawl and the medieval city centre. The tourists who flock around Bologna's great museums and the famous Fountain of Neptune are absent from its southern neighbour. When you walk along the cobbles of Marzabotto, you are alone with the ghosts of the Etruscans, in their city that once called itself Kainua.[3]

The streets themselves are reminiscent of the better-known preserved Roman cities at Pompeii and Herculaneum, preserved by Vesuvius in minute detail. They are rutted with wheel marks, and in the central street are the iconic stepping stones, enabling pedestrians to cross safely, yet still allowing cart access. These symbols of city life are far older than their more famous southern counterparts. At Marzabotto, however, it was an eruption of aggression, not a volcano, which caused the abandonment of a once thriving city. Sacked by marauding Gauls in the middle of the fourth century, the site provides a snapshot into just over a century of Etruscan city life.[4] First constructed in the fifth century BCE, this was a particular kind of town: a colony. It was built at a time of confidence and prosperity, as Etruscan influence spread north and south. As such, it was a new town, designed to an ideal plan: Marzabotto gives an idea of what the perfect Etruscan city should look like. It is built along a grid pattern, avoiding the warren of lanes and streets that characterized so many medieval cities. The houses and streets form neat blocks, just as in later Roman towns.[5]

The excavators at Marzabotto have worked steadily and tirelessly through each of these city blocks, known as 'insulae'. Each rectangular block, divided by minor roads, measured approximately 250 x 30 m, resulting in long, thin building plots. These insulae spread out from a central street, which ran from north to south through the centre of the town. There were three further main roads, all of which intersected this main street. All of these four major route-ways measured 15 m across – wide thoroughfares befitting the major arteries of a bustling city. In its design and planning, Marzabotto has a great deal in common with other Etruscan colonies, like Spina on the Adriatic Coast. The individual houses of Marzabotto are neat and well organized, and remain visible to the modern visitor. The shape of each house survives as its foundations. You can see the layout of the walls and the rooms, feel the flow of movement through each building. The walls themselves are long gone beyond their bases, as are the roofs of these dwellings, long since fallen in. The remnants of the latter survive as garish orange terracotta pieces, fragments with distinct shapes and angles. The system here was the same as that at Poggio Civitate and across the ancient world: two rectangular tiles shaped like long oven trays, covered by a semi-cylindrical tube, open at the bottom, to cover the join. If you look carefully, you can still spot fragments

View of the remains of the Etruscan town of Marzabotto.

of these ubiquitous signs of Etruscan occupation beneath your feet as you wander the streets. Fun as it is to spot the remains of roof tiles, the less obvious finds from the houses beneath them are even more interesting.

One in particular, in Insula II, has been beautifully excavated and lovingly published in exacting detail.[6] In shape, it is similar to all the other homes in the ancient city, and it is designed in a style we are more familiar with from the later Roman world. There is an elegant courtyard garden with what seems to have been an open roof, an early version of the more famous Roman peristylum.[7] Instead of a central pool, however, the majority of the Etruscan inhabitants of Marzabotto enjoyed access to their own wells, and a fresh supply of drinking water in the comfort of their own home.[8] Around the courtyard was a series of rooms, some public, others private. Those nearest the street were peppered with small finds, indicating their function as spaces for work – the debris associated with metalworking and the production of ceramics. At the rear of the house is domestic space, presumably reserved for the family and invited guests only. With these individual water supplies for each house and terracotta guttering to channel rainwater, the people of Marzabotto enjoyed the very latest in interior and exterior design.

The houses are regular in their size and layout, and there are very few signs of the social inequality that is so obvious at Poggio Civitate. This is a space inhabited by what we might call citizens: people of a solid, shared status, living similar lives in their own little town. It is faintly reminiscent of modern Euro-American suburbia, a world of immaculate lawns and identikit homes. It is distinctly at odds with the perceived enigma of the Etruscans. The inhabitants of Marzabotto, in their seemingly petit bourgeois existence, defy the stereotype of the lost civilization, the mysterious Etruscan. They are eminently knowable. The town contains more familiar ingredients: a place of worship, in the form of a large temple dedicated to the god Tinia, the Etruscan equivalent of the Greek god Zeus, king of the gods.[9] Only recently, new buildings have emerged as part of this temple complex, including what is thought to have been a treasury and a structure that may have been a formal dining area for celebratory feasts, known as a hestiatorion.[10] The temple itself slots neatly into the blocks of the city. Unlike temples in new towns built by Greek colonists, it was clearly important to these Etruscan builders that their place of worship be a part of the town. This area around the temple looks suspiciously like public space, an area for the community to gather together – a key feature of any city. It is impossible to be sure that political arguments took place here, as they did in the Roman Forum or the Athenian Agora. But if the inhabitants of Marzabotto needed to come together, to debate, to decide, it is the entirely logical location.

The problem with Marzabotto is its perfection. The discovery of a boulder from the river, marked with a cross and aligned with the cardinal points beneath the main street, emphasizes the careful planning that went into its construction. There is a suggestion that the entire layout was designed to fit with a religious ideal of a city, with Marzabotto's orientation adhering to a blueprint laid out by priests.[11] Although there was a small settlement of huts here prior to the immaculately organized city,[12] the grand sweep of development that transformed Marzabotto in the fifth century sets it apart. Even the name of the city may signify its status as a novelty; some archaeologists believe that the name Kainua is linked to the Greek word *kainos*, meaning 'new', making the ancient name of Marzabotto the equivalent of 'Newtown'.[13] Other colonies preserve the same ideals of town planning and similarly sized dwellings; but are they typical of the Etruscan city, and at what point can we describe Etruscan towns as cities at all?

This question is important, because it is central to our definition of civilization: *civis*, city, is in the very word itself. If the Etruscans had cities, they are instantly on a par with their Greek competitors and Roman successors in our minds. To the classical Greeks, city life was at the heart of their sense of identity. Plato, writing fifty years after the foundation of Marzabotto, devotes much of his masterwork *The Republic* (*c.* 360 BCE) to the ideal design of the city. Indeed, the title of his work in the original Greek is *Politeia*, referencing the city-state, or *polis*. Speaking through the mouth of his mentor Socrates, Plato laid out his views on what makes the city. For him, it begins with the need for people to specialize, to do what they are good at. This results in a community growing as different individuals provide for one another. As it grows, there is the eventual need for a special kind of people, who organize and referee the others, preventing disputes and keeping the peace. They are defined as soldiers and as rulers – those who uphold power through violence and through effective decision-making that engenders respect. With these special 'guardians' in charge, everyone else can get on with doing 'one's own business' and avoid being a 'busybody'.[14] Plato goes on further, outlining an extreme society in which, to avoid injustice, children are raised outside their birth families and it is the rulers who decide which couples are to marry. This disturbing vision is a leap from the original observations of *The Republic*, a strange reversal from the more pragmatic vision of everyone getting on with their own affairs without interference. What begins as a definition of a city turns into a dystopian nightmare.

Aristotle, too, in the fourth century BCE, took up the issue of what makes a city. Rather than presenting a debate between philosophers, Aristotle chose to critique the work of a practical man, perhaps the first professional town planner.[15] Hippodamus was born in Miletus, one of the Greek cities on the coast of what is now Turkey. Prior to its invasion by the Persians, Miletus was one of the most respected (and richest) cities of the Greek universe. In 499 BCE, as punishment for the citizens' involvement in a rebellion, Miletus was seriously damaged by Persian forces. It began a steady recovery, and Hippodamus, as architect, was deeply involved in its redesign. He would go on to work in Piraeus, the port of Athens, and in Italy. His central tenet is the division of the city into three forms of space: public, private and religious.[16] It is Hippodamus who is credited with the idea of the grid plan, incorporating all three forms of space into one harmonious whole. Hippodamus, like Plato, had clear ideas on what types of citizen his perfect *polis* should contain: soldiers, craftspeople and farmers. Sceptical and suspicious, Aristotle disagreed – he felt that all inhabitants of a city (that is, all male inhabitants) should fulfil all these tasks, lest the soldiers become corrupted by power and rule by violence. By extension, Aristotle also criticized Plato's preference for specialism:

his philosopher guardians are as problematic as Hippodamus' armed guards. Aristotle was not above a few catty comments about Hippodamus, too, describing him as having 'long hair, expensive ornaments, and the same cheap warm clothing worn summer and winter'.[17]

He sounds like the prototype of the eccentric architect. But the Hippodamian ideal of urban planning, if not of government, remains with us today – in the endless roundabouts of Milton Keynes, in the careful grid plan of New York. It can certainly be seen in many Roman cities, and in forts from the Syrian Desert to Hadrian's Wall. The Roman adoption of Hippodamian principles spread this form of the city far and wide, and their language provided us with the word we continue to use for this particular kind of urban centre: city, *cité*, *città*. They all originate from the Latin word *civis* and its associated term, *civitas*. These two words are important, as they wrap together the people who live in a place and the place itself. *Civis* is best translated as citizen: a person who dwells within a particular urban centre. It is the second term, *civitas*, that elevated the Roman citizen above their Samnite or Gaulish neighbour. *Civitas* is the law, the system of government that unites the people. In many ways, it is the ideological incarnation of Plato's guardians, protecting the community from outsiders and from themselves by laying down behavioural boundaries within physical ones.

However, unlike the idea of the philosophical guardians of Plato, *civitas* enshrines all the free inhabitants of a city as their *own* protectors. Their will and their desire for a peaceful existence glue together the disparate interests of individuals and households. Indeed, the legendary origin of the term comes from the weaving together of two Italic peoples into one community: the moment at which the Sabines and Romans became one.[18] *Civitas*, then, is a contract between all those who live in a particular city. It lays out the responsibilities that all members of the community have towards each other, and the rights of protection that they can expect from one another. In Rome, as in classical Athens for a brief period, the enforcement of the law was provided by elected officials. Magistrates of different statuses had varying levels of power: from local lawgivers all the way up to the highest consuls.[19] The Roman orator Cicero, who died in the middle of the first century BCE, was himself an elected consul and provides a more detailed vision of the way the *civitas* should function.[20] It should act to balance the diverse powers of the mob and the wealthy. It should be independent and unbiased, not favouring any particular faction. It gives rights to each and every citizen, which are not to be enjoyed by outsiders. Its status should be bestowed at the moment of birth, and only end with death or exile. It is the ultimate standard of behaviour. It is what makes city life worth living.

So, from the Greek and Roman sources, we can draw out two crucial aspects that define a city. How do they sit with the archaeological evidence from Marzabotto, and from the urban centres of the Etruscans? The first, developed from Plato and (more significantly) from Hippodamus, is focused upon space. Are the three key types of space to be found within Etruscan towns and, as such, can they be described as cities? At Marzabotto, they certainly are. The houses of the people are immaculately organized. The temple provides a space for worship, and adjacent to it is an area that looks suspiciously like a gathering place. It is remarkable that even as Hippodamus was working in Greece, the same principles of organization were used to mark out this town on the edge of the Apennines. Nor is the presence of these different kinds of space unique to Marzabotto. Excavations at Tarquinia demonstrate the presence of a temple from the earliest phase of occupation. At San Giovenale, another southern site, by the sixth century we can see the prototypes of the courtyard house, with neat wells and cisterns. Indeed, at the nearby site of Acquarossa there is evidence for geometric town planning that certainly pre-dates its 'invention' by Hippodamus.[21] Marzabotto is an exceptional survival, but not a unique phenomenon. Public, private and religious spaces: check. By this measure, at least, the Etruscan town must be acknowledged as a city.

The problem comes with the second block that builds the definition of a city: the formalized social contract that exists in formal terms as *civitas*. Any community has rules, or it fails to function. However, this specific form of citizenship, in which each member of the community is involved and invested in the running of a city, and which is enshrined in a formal declaration of rights and responsibilities, is more difficult to find in the archaeological record. The neat streets and well-kept spaces of Marzabotto certainly argue for some form of municipal power, but can we detect a formal contract in place here? It is perhaps best to approach this question sideways: what are the associated trappings of a *civitas*-style system of city governance? One of the major features of the Roman model is the existence of elected magistrates, and these we may be able to detect in Etruria. Certainly, individuals are depicted in art with the trappings of later magisterial power: notably a particular kind of staff with a curved head, the *lituus*. However, this could be a symbol of straightforward feudal control, not the possession of power on behalf of the population.[22]

In the Etruscan language the word for magistrate is *zilath*. We find this word engraved on tomb markers from the site of Rubiera, north of Marzabotto, dating to the late seventh century.[23] So, the position of magistrate was in place just as Etruscan settlements began to expand to a size commensurate with physical definitions of the city. That the term continues to be used on tombstones into the third century illustrates the longevity of the office, and its importance to the structure of Etruscan society. Further inscriptions give other scraps of information: a bronze weight from the southern city of Cerveteri inscribed with the name of a magistrate hints that these individuals were in charge of weights and measures within their cities, ensuring honest dealings among traders.[24] Another inscription, cut into a road, records that a *marun*, or specialized magistrate, called Larth Lapicanes supervized construction.[25] So there is evidence for public works, and for specialized roles within the magistracy, from at least the early fifth century BCE, as towns were expanding. Qualifying adjectives such as *marun* and the as yet untranslated *eterau* delineated exactly which kind of *zilath* you were dealing with. It is impossible to conclusively pin the highly specific Roman concept of *civitas* on to Etruscan urban living. Yet it seems unlikely that a similar agreement between citizens, and potentially a system of elected magistrates, was not in place here.

The Greek and Roman definitions of a city are deliberately structured. Part observation, part inspiration, they flatter the status quo while seeking to improve it still further. Both Plato and Cicero were convinced of the superiority of their own socio-political systems, and of their potential to become even better. These authors set the tone for any debate over what a city should be, and formed the idea of a city in the image of Athens and Rome. Any city built and run by an alien culture by definition could not form part of this model. Yet, as we have seen, at Marzabotto and elsewhere, there is substantial evidence that this type of urban living was common in Etruria: indeed, that it was central to Etruscan identity. Just as the word *zilath* illustrates a complex and sophisticated system of bureaucracy, justice and public works, so the word *Rasenna* prompts a new idea of what it meant to be Etruscan. This word can be shortened to *Rasna*, or *Raśna* (pronounced rash-na). It is the word the Etruscans used to describe themselves, the word that delineates insiders, members of their society. And what does *Rasenna*/*Rasna*/*Raśna* mean? It means people of the city.[26]

Taking the Etruscans at their own estimation, then, we have a people whose commitment to urban life was so central to their existence it defined them as a group. It also provides an insight into their values, their preferences, the experiences they wanted to build their lives from. By the end of the Archaic period, after a time of boom and bust, life in cities like Marzabotto was the explicit norm for an Etruscan person. It offered security, safety, prosperity. The idealized design speaks of spreading influence and wealth – the resources to build a new centre from scratch and fill it with people, all equally committed to the same lifestyle. That lifestyle was vastly different from the villages of only a few centuries before, and a world away from the unbalanced rural palaces of Poggio Civitate.

Think of the extraordinary variation in experience between town and country life: the hum of people moving through the streets, talking, laughing; babies and children shrieking and giggling; drunks at night, traders in the morning, your neighbours on both sides arguing at all hours; the unavoidable smells of people living together – the rubbish and human waste, but also the tantalizing odours of food cooking, the waft of perfumed oil coming off someone's skin; the sense of safety and security that comes from sharing space with many other people; the satisfaction of working together for a new road; the frustration with a poor magistrate; the little arguments and triumphs that made up each individual Etruscan existence. A walk along the main street of Marzabotto brings this home like nothing else.

In the later history of Marzabotto, a dark chapter serves as a final reminder of what can happen when the power of the state turns against the people, when the philosophy of city life and guardianship is an evil one. This quiet place was the site of one of the worst atrocities to take place in Italy during the Second World War. The area around Marzabotto, the combination of high hills and proximity to the major city of Bologna, made it a hotbed of partisan activity. The local people largely supported the growing Resistance, who were becoming increasingly bold. The bigwigs of the Bologna Fascists were their targets, and they included an Etruscan specialist, Pericle Ducati (1880–1944). Ducati was delighted to co-opt the Etruscans into Mussolini's reimagining of the Italian past. He was convinced that Etruscan cultural glories reflected the innate genius of the Italian people.[27] Ducati's warped pride in Etruscan culture won him archaeological awards, but also a position as a prominent Fascist politician. He signed the infamous Manifesto of Fascist Intellectuals in 1925, and by the 1940s, in addition to being the director of the Museo Civico of Bologna, he was sitting in judgement as a bastion of the Fascist establishment. It was this fateful combination of roles that killed him.

Bronze perfume dipper, potentially belonging to a man or a woman of the 4th century. Not from Marzabotto, it is a reminder of the importance of scent in the Etruscan world.

On the morning of 16 February 1944, Ducati was shot by partisans while leaving his home on the way to work. The partisans fled on a bicycle, vanishing into the backstreets of the city. Ducati is thought to have been targeted due to his role as a figurehead, and as a judge, hated for passing sentences on partisans fighting for Italian freedom. After the fall of Mussolini, Bologna lay in the German-controlled area of northern Italy, and in continuing to serve as a judge, Ducati was acting as a puppet for the Nazis,

Late Etruscan cista with cover – again, not from Marzabotto but a potentially important personal possession.

turning over his countrymen to the cruelties of the occupying power. It was for their murdered comrades that the two bicycle assassins struck. Their audacious raid left Ducati gravely wounded, and after months of suffering he died in October that year. The late summer and autumn of 1944 was marked by many such executions, and the regional SS commander, Walter Reder, determined to act.

Between 29 September and 5 October, Reder led his men into the mountains around Marzabotto, now the Monte Sole historic park. Men, women and children were rounded up and systematically slaughtered. The horror spared no one: 45 victims were infants aged under two, and a further 205 children under sixteen were murdered. One of the village priests, Giovanni Fornasini, managed to spirit away as many of his parishioners as he could, but was himself slain. The total number of people killed remains unclear. The accepted number is 770 villagers murdered in Marzabotto, with others from the nearby villages of Monzuno and Grizzana Morandi included in the massacre.[28] As one of the most extreme war crimes in Europe of the Second World War, the massacre continues to cast a dark shadow over the village. The museum itself was severely damaged by bombs and shellfire, its exhibits charred and destroyed.[29] This town, this mountain haven begun by the Etruscans, could not protect its inhabitants from violence, past and present. The role of a town is to protect and provide for a community. The role of a state is to take good care of its citizens, treating them equally and with justice. When these twin roles fail, the people will suffer. As the Etruscans seem to have realized, city living comes at a social price – and continues to do so.

The so-called 'Cannicella Venus' of Orvieto.

EIGHT
SEX, LIES AND ETRUSCANS

Deep in inland Umbria, a dramatic outcrop of rock is crowned by a walled town: Orvieto. In its central piazza is a spectacular medieval cathedral. Its golden facade glints in the sun, reflecting the light back into a museum dedicated to the town's ancient residents. The Museo Claudio Faina is filled with Etruscan treasures, including a rather unusual statue. The statue is of a woman, and she is entirely nude. Her surviving hand gestures to her pubis, the other arm and her left breast are missing. So too are her adornments, their presence attested to only by cuts in the marble: holes for the ears, and the removal of some hair to allow for a diadem. A nude female statue might not seem strange to our eyes: we are accustomed to nude female statuary. Yet this statue is entirely unique. It is made of marble from the Greek islands but no contemporary Greek statue has yet been found that shows a woman in such utter nakedness.[1]

The statue has had a tempestuous journey from its original form as a block of marble on an Aegean island.[2] It seems to have been originally carved in the style of the famous *kouros* figures, nude youths found all over the Greek world. However, any male apparatus was carefully removed, and two new breasts were added, carved in matching marble and attached to the torso. The suggestion of a vulva was created, and while the face remains reminiscent of other *kouroi*, its lips are fuller, its eyes larger. Creating this statue must have been a strange and discomforting experience for the probably Greek craftspeople who carved it. While male *kouroi* are regularly and cheerfully naked, their female equivalents, *kore*, are always clothed. Always. This female figure was made to order for an Etruscan audience that wanted their statue nude. Presumably, they were willing to pay for this preference – a made-to-order marble statue, just under a metre in height, would not have come cheap. Perhaps it was while on the journey from Greece that the statue was damaged: she was repaired in antiquity, with the surviving breast and both legs in need of attention.[3]

On arrival in Orvieto, the statue found a home just outside the town, in what seems to have been a religious complex. One of the finest surviving Etruscan temples, that of the Belvedere, is to be found just outside the funicular station in Orvieto, but this statue was installed in the area of the Cannicella sanctuary and its associated necropolis: that is, at the bottom of the cliff to the south of the town. The statue was not indoors, hidden away from sight: weathering on the marble suggests that this female body was on display outside, exposed to both the elements and the eyes of anyone visiting the necropolis.[4] The sanctuary and necropolis have been excavated extensively, and the statue was found *in situ*, outside two buildings but close to what seems to have been a round pool, and perhaps an associated altar.[5] The sanctuary was founded in the late sixth century BCE, with the statue arriving around 520, or a little later. Expansion in the fourth century meant the religious area outgrew its original boundaries, with older tombs sacrificed to make way for ritual space. With the constant use of the site, even into the Roman period, it is no surprise that the golden jewellery is long gone. That the statue itself survived in position is a rare and precious thing. The 'Cannicella Venus' is named both for the necropolis she was found in and the Roman goddess of desire. The two halves of this nickname do not fit easily together: why would a deity connected with love and sex be with the dead? Is it appropriate to see a sexualization of this nude figure? Why was it acceptable in Etruscan society to view a woman's body entirely unclothed?

This is far from the most shocking vision of a woman's body to be found in the context of Etruscan burials. At Tarquinia, the visitor can descend into the earth to view more surprising, and disturbing, scenes. This time, they are painted on tomb walls, seemingly hidden from view. However, these tombs would have been entered, and the images encountered, time and again by mourners. Following in their footsteps down this particular tomb's entrance corridor, a disturbing image looms out of the dark. It's a deeply uncomfortable scene. A woman is bent over between two men, both of whom are beating her. One has oral sex, the other vaginal sex, with her. These figures give the tomb its name – The Tomb of the Whipping – but they are not alone. Next to them is another group of three – again, two men and a woman who stands between them. There are other, comparable images of sex in Etruscan tombs, including another in this very cemetery. The Tomb of the Bulls, one of the oldest painted tombs here, contains a series of participants having sex in a variety of positions. In this case it is clear that some of these couples are two male figures, while others are male and female. There is also a group of three – a woman balanced on the back of a man on all fours, being penetrated by a standing male. There are also images of male lovemaking in the Tomb of the Bigas, where a couple have intercourse underneath what seems to be a grandstand.[6]

With other examples of sexual behaviour in Etruscan burial contexts, perhaps the sexualization of the statue from Cannicella is unavoidable? It would certainly seem to fit with one aspect of the Etruscan legend. This particular legend is most visible in museum gift shops across Etruria: at Tarquinia, and in Orvieto, where phallic keyrings and guides to the eroticism of the Etruscans are available. The smirking sexualization of the Etruscans belies the rareness of explicitly sexual images, and in particular their position alongside the respected dead. How have we travelled from images of lovemaking, sexualized violence and a unique, beautiful statue, to a sniggering legacy with overtones of 'bunga bunga'?

The classical sources are the origin point for this unpleasant aspect of the Etruscan legend. The most vicious account is that of the fourth century BCE Theopompus of Chios:

> Sharing wives is an established Etruscan custom. Etruscan women take particular care of their bodies and exercise often, sometimes along with the men, and sometimes by themselves. It is not a disgrace for them to be seen naked. They do not share

> their couches with their husbands but with the other men who happen to be present, and they propose toasts to anyone they choose. They are expert drinkers and very attractive.
>
> The Etruscans raise all the children that are born, without knowing who their fathers are. The children live the way their parents live, often attending drinking parties and having sexual relations with all the women. It is no disgrace for them to do anything in the open, or to be seen having it done to them, for they consider it a native custom. . . .
>
> When they are having sexual relations either with courtesans or within their family, they do as follows: after they have stopped drinking and are about to go to bed, while the lamps are still lit, servants bring in courtesans, or boys, or sometimes even their wives. . . . They sometimes make love and have intercourse while people are watching them, but most of the time they put screens woven of sticks around the beds, and throw cloths on top of them.
>
> They are keen on making love to women, but they particularly enjoy boys and youths. The youths in Etruria are very good-looking, because they live in luxury and keep their bodies smooth. In fact all the barbarians in the West use pitch to pull out and shave off the hair on their bodies.[7]

On the face of it, there are themes in Theopompus' account that we might be tempted to connect with the imagery from Tarquinia, and to a sexualized goddess at Orvieto. The representation of sex alongside formal banquets certainly fits with his description. So does the acceptability of sex in public: if it is 'no disgrace . . . to do anything in the open' then we can assume that it is no disgrace to represent anything either. Also, a number of the Etruscan revellers are portrayed with a lack of body hair, perhaps as a result of pitch-based waxing. If Theopompus is correct in this detail, is it feasible to accept his account of Etruscan sexual habits in general, and slot the 'Cannicella Venus' and the frescoes of the Tomb of the Whipping into a libertine lifestyle? The story of his life, and the tale of this text's survival, is essential in assessing the truth of Theopompus' account.

The kind of Etruscan black-figure vase painting that perpetuates the myth of hypersexualized Etruscans.

Having spent his childhood on Chios, Theopompus headed to Athens. Shortly afterwards, he was exiled with his father, who sympathized with the Spartan side in the aftermath of the Peloponnesian War (431–404 BCE). Theopompus went on to become an accomplished orator and historian, supported first by Alexander the Great and later by Ptolemy, ending his life in Egypt.[8] It was here that the Graeco-Egyptian author Athenaeus of Naucratis pulled together the attendees of his dream dinner party, bringing together texts from thinkers he admired in fifteen books of curated conversation. Athenaeus' work, the *Deipnosophistae*, or 'Dinner with the Experts', was produced in the early third century CE. So, there is a serious problem with the chronology of these different stories. Think of the changes to sexual attitudes in Euro-American culture between the 1910s and the 2010s regarding same-sex marriage, extramarital sex, divorce and abortion.

In addition to the chronological distance between Theopompus' surviving account and the Etruscans he was writing about, there was also geographical distance. It's unclear whether the disapproving Theopompus ever travelled to Italy at all. His account reads as an almost standardized slander of any barbarous nation.[9] The lack of body hair, the effeminacy of men, is levelled against Greek enemies in the East – the Lydians and later Persians.[10] Texts and images of these people show men dressed in loose trousers, with strange helmets and smooth skin. They are depicted as clowns with a hint of menace: their attention to their bodies in a distinctly unmanly way distinguishes them as strange, foreign and dangerous. The use of these same smears to taint the Etruscans seems likely to be redolent more of Greek prejudices than of cultural realities. Equally, the use of eunuchs and the existence of male–male sexual relationships outside the carefully regulated relationship between a young man and older admirer seen as normal in Athens was used to denigrate the Persian foe. In the same collection of Athenaeus' diners as Theopompus' diatribe we hear from Heraclides of Pontus, a fourth-century BCE historian. His life's work was a deeply biased history of Persia, written from the perspective of a Greek living under the Achaemenid Empire. Heracleides provided scintillating details on the sexual lives of Persian kings, who supposedly slept all day to devote their nights to music and sex with royal concubines.[11] Who could respect an empire ruled over by such louche, lazy men?

A similar message lies beneath Theopompus' account of sexual intrigue in Etruria. His point is that the sexual politics of the Etruscans leave them open to rightful conquest. Just as the Persian kings, through their dalliances by night, neglect their kingdom and do not deserve success in battle, so the Etruscans do not own the rights to their lands. Look again at the text: the most shocking element in the scandalous behaviour of the Etruscans is that 'even their wives' supposedly join in sexual play, and euphemistically 'toast' any man they please. What is the result? All the children born are raised equally, however much they might resemble a friend or neighbour. So, from a hostile (and patriarchal) perspective, all Etruscan children may not be the true heirs to their father's possessions. The stain of illegitimacy hovers over the entire population. From this angle, all Etruscan landowners, however much they may flaunt their wealth and privilege, are just bastards, no better than a whore's brat from the gutter. They can be treated by the Greeks who encounter them with snobbish disdain. Worse, the lands of the Etruscans are not rightly theirs – they are forfeit, up for grabs to any Greek who wants to claim them.

Theopompus also seems to have been a man who disapproved of physical pleasure in almost every form; certainly not someone who would make most people's dream dinner party guest list. His time in Athens, learning his trade amid the tumultuous arguments that filled the vacuum left by the great Socrates, moulded Theopompus into a committed anti-hedonist. The philosophy of hedonism argues that the pursuit of pleasure is the only real purpose of life – enjoyment is the only intrinsic goal of living. It was proposed by the philosopher Aristippus (435–356 BCE), a foreigner and native of Cyrene, in what is now Libya. Aristippus reacted instinctively against the Socratic concept of the virtuous life, although he is supposed to have come to Athens specifically to learn from the great man. It is possible that his violent reaction against Socratic principles resulted from Aristippus' time with his idol: having witnessed the downfall of his master in spite of his apparent virtues, Aristippus instead determined to have a good time. Other heirs of Socrates' thought were disgusted at this attitude, and among these puritanical thinkers was a young Theopompus. One of the major charges levelled against Aristippus was his sexual behaviour: he moved in with a beautiful hetaera (the term means 'companion' but refers to a skilled professional courtesan), Lais. Theopompus could not have failed to be influenced by this environment of sexualized politics, personal distrust of pleasure and vicious slander.[12] It is these problematic ingredients that lie behind this most famous account of Etruscan sexuality.

From this perspective, it seems obvious that Theopompus' writings should be dismissed as biased. Perhaps they do reflect some small aspects of Etruscan behaviour; the presence of women at banquets, for instance, is supported by the archaeological record. There is no way, however, of recording what might have happened after such a dinner between a couple, between friends, or between an owner and slaves; no way of proving that Theopompus was wrong. When the Greek sources are put together with the misbehaviour of elite Etruscan women and the sexual appropriation of another man's wife described in the Roman literature, the relative ambiguity of the archaeological record becomes a space for the imagination. Interpretation can be coloured by ancient texts, but also by the personal preferences and perceptions of an individual viewer. Certainly, the eighteenth-century critique of Etruscan art by Winckelmann implies a hypersexuality which denigrates their style of work. The bulging muscles, leaping women, exaggerated eyes and lips – they all contribute to a swaggering sexuality that is seen as infusing and undermining the Etruscan artistic achievement.

While the sexual morality of the Etruscans was a turn-off for Winckelmann, it was part of the appeal for another artist and pleasure-lover. This man is probably responsible for the majority of popular perceptions of the Etruscans, at least in Britain. He is also responsible for folded corners on pages in books across the world, and a landmark court case. David Herbert Lawrence was born in 1885, the son of a coal miner and a former teacher. The young Lawrence benefitted from his mother's thwarted teaching career, winning a scholarship to secondary school and eventually qualifying as a teacher himself. His writing flourished through intense relationships with women; a friend lent him her personal diaries, he proposed to and jilted a childhood friend, and suffered deep grief after the death of his mother.[13] In 1912, however, he met the love of his life. Unfortunately, she was already married.

Frieda Weekley's beauty shines out from portraits, with even features and wide, knowing eyes beneath richly piled hair. Six years Lawrence's senior, she already had three children when she eloped with the young writer. The pair escaped to Germany, Frieda's native land, before journeying south to Italy for the first time. Lawrence would return to the country again and again, exploring different regions, including stays on the Tuscan coast, in Sicily near Taormina, and the mountains of Abruzzo. In between these visits, his life remained tumultuous; the relationship with Frieda excluded him from polite society, while the First World War's tensions between Britain and Germany exacerbated their already difficult social position. In 1925 Lawrence moved back to Tuscany, taking up residence in a villa near Florence. It was here that he wrote his most infamous work, *Lady Chatterley's Lover*, which was first published privately in Florence.

In the spring of 1927, the year before the publication of *Lady Chatterley*, Lawrence headed south to the most famous Etruscan sites, including Tarquinia. The sites were deserted, accessed from strange and eerie stations in the middle of nowhere. Lawrence spent a month exploring in the company of local guides, who he would later caricature. His adventures are recounted in *Sketches of Etruscan Places* (1932), a series of vignettes which remains a beloved piece of travel literature. Each visit is described in typical, lyrical style, and Lawrence turns description to a philosophy of living, as here in his description of sarcophagi from Tarquinia:

> If it is a man, his body is exposed to just below the navel, and he holds in his hand the sacred patera . . . which represents the round germ of heaven and earth . . . So within each man is the quick of him, when he is a baby, and when he is old, the same quick; some spark, some unborn and undying life-electron.[14]

Whether translating sculpture into the meaning of life or daydreaming about the Etruscan roots of people he met on the bus, Lawrence was in love with his vision of the Etruscans. In his vision, they reflect all the values and virtues he holds dear. To him, their art shows a lost world in which sexual enjoyment is without shame – it is the same utopian world of which Constance dreams in the arms of Mellors. The Cannicella statue and the Tomb of the Whipping were not discovered until the 1960s, at the start of another sexual revolution, so we will never know what Lawrence would have thought of them. It is possible to make an educated guess, however, based on his emotive response to another image from Tarquinia. Here he is on the Tomb of the Triclinium, which he renamed the Tomb of the Feast:

> And how lovely these have been, and still are! The band of dancing figures that go round the room still is bright in colour, fresh . . . wildly the bacchic woman throws back her head and curves out her long strong fingers, wild and yet contained within herself, while the broad-bodied young man turns round to her, lifting his dancing hand to hers till the thumbs all but touch.[15]

The Cannicella statue, her rounded breasts and sleek flanks, would probably have moved Lawrence to fits of ecstasy – the expression of what he would doubtless choose to interpret as consensual sexual exploration in the public space of death would have confirmed his view of the healthy openness of Etruscan society. Beneath the travelogue style of *Etruscan Places* is a manifesto and a warning. The book contrasts the freedom and beauty of Etruscan life (including what Lawrence interprets as sexual liberation) with the Italy he travelled through. Mussolini, who identified his regime with the glory of Rome, is portrayed as heir to the Roman evil which destroyed the Etruscans, even as fascism would tear Europe apart. Lawrence is scornful of the militarism and propaganda of both ancient and fascist Rome; he dismisses Roman accounts of the Etruscans which undermine his personal interpretation. The path to happiness is the reconstruction of Etruscan values – the pursuit of pleasure in all its forms.

Fifth-century decoration from a candelabra showing a couple embracing.

This might seem like a spirited riposte to the attack of Theopompus. However, by interpreting Etruscan archaeology to suit his own personal story, Lawrence propped up the description of Etruscan life as louche. He unwittingly supported the criticisms and slanders of hostile authors by choosing to recast, rather than refute, them. If your most vocal supporter in the English language is a famed reprobate, it won't do your reputation any good. Through the twentieth century, with the discovery of the Tomb of the Whipping and recognition of other sexual images in Etruscan art, Theopompus' account and Lawrence's recasting of it have been absorbed into public preconceptions of the Etruscans. The interpretation of the Cannicella statue as a love-goddess presiding over her people is certainly an interpretation born of free love.

The problem is that the Cannicella figure, and the erotic tomb paintings, are remarkable precisely because they are rare. The trappings of Etruscan sexual culture are well hidden, unlike their counterparts in Athens. There, in spite of the fulminations of Theopompus and friends, the controlled relationships between young and older men, husbands and wives, prostitutes and customers made the rules of sexual play highly visible. Their representation in art and literature was inevitable. In Etruria, we do not know which kinds of relationships were encouraged, and which were looked down on. We do not know the extent to which consent was enshrined in codes of sexual behaviour. This lack of knowledge has created a void, into which Theopompus, Lawrence, Winckelmann and the Tarquinia gift shop have inserted their view of the sex lives of the Etruscans. And of course, sex sells, especially when flavoured with a delightful hint of scandal. Is it any surprise, then, that this aspect of the Etruscan myth is so strong that new finds, even of a beautiful nude goddess in a burial ground, are instantly pulled down into the pit?

In the face of this ideology, what alternative interpretation could we suggest for the strange juxtaposition of sex and death that the Cannicella figure seems to present? In the case of the Cannicella figure, later finds have added a little more evidence for her identity. The sanctuary seems to have been dedicated to a goddess named as Vei.[16] This is not the Etruscan equivalent of Aphrodite or Venus – her name is Turan. Vei seems to have been more closely linked to fertility of the land, and presumably of the people, based on the discovery of inscriptions to her and to the Greek goddess Demeter in the same place. The connection with fertility is the beginning of an explanation for the presence of a nude statue in a necropolis that does not rely on tropes of hypersexualization. Perhaps we might look also at the experience of sex, and the 'little death' of orgasm. While this term is obviously a recent one, the transformative nature of intercourse is undeniable. Like any ritual, there is a before, during and after: three states in which a number of things are irrevocably transformed. The bodies of the participants, their relationship with one another, potentially the creation of a child but certainly the transfer of bodily fluids: all are changed. Death, too, is a transformation of bodies and relationships. It too takes three stages. It too is irrevocable. The funeral context, the need for hope for the future in the face of bereavement and grief, is a perfect position for a comforting goddess who is dedicated to both sex and death.

In this context, the Cannicella statue should not be shocking or out of place. It is our own perceptions that make us react in this way. Throughout this chapter we have seen the ways in which Etruscan sexuality has been recast by outsiders to suit their specifications. Theopompus needed to tarnish a rival power. Winckelmann needed to explain his disdain for previously lauded Etruscan artworks. Lawrence needed to channel his own desires and fears into a dream of a lost world. The Etruscan scholars of the 1960s needed to explain their finds, turning to the shifting society in which they lived for inspiration. The stockists of the Tarquinia and Orvieto museum gift shops know that visitors will be enthralled by tales of sexual mischief. Yet those same visitors' interest in sex in print, sex on film and sex in the past is matched by fear: fear of death and fear of oblivion. For us, it feels alien and inappropriate to bring these two monumental forces together: better to laugh at one, and try to forget about the other. Perhaps the Etruscan acceptance of the centrality and interrelatedness of sex and death is a healthier response to both.

Mirror showing Paris and Helen, Achilles and Chryseis, all identified by their Etruscan names, 3rd century.

NINE
Wrapped Up Writings

In picking up this book, and turning to this page, you are performing a remarkable trick. It's a relatively recent skill, putting together some of the most powerful abilities of the human brain. You are able to look at these black and white shapes of print, and string them together. They make words. The words make ideas. I can communicate another world to you through these words, describing places you have perhaps never seen. When we stop to think about writing, and reading, it is an absolutely remarkable phenomenon that transforms lives. The emergence of literacy, and latterly mass literacy, has had a huge impact on the world. Modern digital technologies are all based upon text, whether acres of plain script on Wikipedia or the swaddled layers of code that underlie each website. Emojis and textspeak reduce this form of visual communication to its purest form, returning to the pictographs where written language began.

Throughout this book, writing has been important. Descriptions of the Etruscans by other people have survived only because they were committed to wax, papyrus or vellum and then carefully stored and jealously guarded. These are the lucky ones, freakish survivors usually from a rarefied world. The vast majority of historical texts were written by wealthy men, in a position of great privilege, often acknowledged as wise and worthy of having their words remembered. The words of women, and of poor people, survive incredibly rarely. The Vindolanda tablets are one of the exceptions to this rule.[1] Carefully recovered from the waterlogged soil of the north of England, they record the everyday minutiae of

Carnelian ring with Etruscan inscription naming Kapaneus (Capne) struck by Zeus' thunderbolt.

Roman lives in this fort just south of Hadrian's Wall. Now, the words of women inviting each other to parties and soldiers writing home to ask for fresh socks have pride of place in the British Museum. These letters are special not only for their rarity and the information they provide about life in Roman Britain; they are important evidence for the flowering of mass literacy.

There is no equivalent to the Vindolanda tablets from Etruria. Instead, there is an awkward vacuum. Etruscan texts exist. Go to almost any Etruscan archaeological site and you'll find something with writing on: an inscription carved into stone, or scrawled on a pot. The letters are clear and easy to read: an alphabet derived from a mixture of Greek and Phoenician scripts from the Eastern Mediterranean.[2] You work from right to left, unpicking each letter. And what do you get? A name, another name, a relationship between the names, maybe a descriptive adjective or two on a good day. That's it. You can glean a great deal from these scraps of information, and scholars of the Etruscans have had to do this. You can trace families, realize that a mother and a father are named and argue for the importance of women in Etruscan society. You can spot a term like *zilath,* and infer an Etruscan kind of *civitas.* There is, however, no equivalent of Livy's *History of Rome*. No Plato, and his idealized *Republic*. Certainly no gossip about the neighbours across the Mediterranean, in the style of Theopompus of Chios. Instead, there is more or less silence.

This is one of the central features of the legend of the Etruscans as unknowable and strange. It is hard to feel distant from the two societies of Greece and Rome, which underlie so much of Western culture. That dominance comes from the texts that survived, squirrelled away in monasteries, to survive invaders and zealots alike. Rising again in the fifteenth and sixteenth centuries as the world was reforged, these texts underpinned the development of European power and eventually became justification for empires that spanned the globe. The power of classical texts continues to compel. These words, scrawled down so long ago, have lost none of their ability to impress, acting as ambassadors for the societies which originally produced them. It isn't just serious treatises that have given these cultures their elevated position in our consciousness; artistic expression has a deep pull of familiarity too, perhaps more important than any serious-minded science or philosophy. If you sit down to read the poems of Ovid or Sappho, what strikes you straight away is just how well-worn the feelings that both writers describe are. The works of any Etruscan poets, however, are totally lost to us.

There are two major reasons for this frustrating situation. The first is that Etruscan scholars wrote their masterpieces on perishable materials. The two most common media seem to have been fragile papyrus scrolls and books made from linen cloth. There are images of both types of literary artefact: you can see Etruscan gods of death carrying scrolls, presumably with the names of the dead inscribed inside. Linen books may be shown in sculpture on a number of items of tomb furniture. One in particular, now in the Vatican, shows the linen book placed so close to the deceased's head that it is almost touching.[3] In the main, however, these materials do not last unless they are deliberately and carefully preserved (or, in some cases, accidentally preserved by a volcanic eruption or quirk of storage environment). Papyrus suffers if it becomes damp, rotting away into oblivion. Repeated folding doesn't help. Linen, too, decays when damp, but is also prey to insect pests. Even where Etruscan texts were stored safely and securely, they could be deliberately destroyed – through burning, tearing or reuse. You can rip up a linen book and recycle its pages very usefully, as the object at the centre of this chapter demonstrates.

The Zagreb text does not look anything like the books we know. Instead, it was cut up into strips and used to bind up the body of a woman, becoming mummy wrappings.[4] Purchased by an adventurous young Croatian, Mihajlo Barić, in 1848, the mummy was a souvenir of his travels in Egypt. Brought to Vienna, the mummy became a talking point, propped upright in the eccentric Barić's living room. At some point, growing curious about his new friend, Barić unwrapped the mummy and stripped away the bandages. It seems that he took the writing for granted; no evidence survives that he tried to call in antiquities experts to examine the wrappings. After Barić died, the mummy and her wrappings were packed off to what was then the Kingdom of Slavonia, now eastern Croatia. She was still in an upright position, secured by an iron rod in a ghoulish display. Her recipient was Barić's brother Ilija, a priest with little interest in his brother's freakish collections. After ten years, the priest had had enough. He signed over possession of Barić's antiquities to the institution that would become the modern Archaeological Museum in Zagreb.

On arrival, the mummy was described for the catalogue, and packed carefully away. The scholar who recorded her arrival noted the presence of the inscriptions, but considered them to be Egyptian hieroglyphics. An expert was called in, all the way from Cairo. Heinrich Brugsch (1827–1894) was a German Egyptologist, who had excavated at Memphis. He was a leading expert in the translation of late Egyptian texts, commencing his work at the precocious age of sixteen, so it is curious that he ignored the markings. It was a chance encounter with a celebrity of the nineteenth century that saved the Zagreb mummy from obscurity in the vaults of the museum. Brugsch had enjoyed a period working in Persia as an ambassador, before being appointed as Prussian consul in Cairo. At some point on his travels he had made the acquaintance of the infamous Richard Burton (1821–1890), the British explorer. It seems likely that the two men met after 1869, when Burton had been posted to Damascus, although they could have encountered each other in Cairo fifteen years before. In 1887 the two men chatted together about runes and scripts, and Brugsch brought up the strange marks on the Zagreb mummy wrappings. Sadly, these two great men concluded that they were remarkably rare . . . examples of the Egyptian *Book of the Dead* in an Arabic script![5]

Fourteen years later, in 1891, the mummy was packed off to Vienna once again. On arrival, the wrappings were examined by Jacob Krall, another expert in late Egyptian texts – this time Coptic. He wanted to examine the perplexing text, expecting it to be a rare form of Coptic, or possibly Libyan, script. Amazingly, it was only at this point that the wrappings were reassembled together, revealing their form: they were recognizably a linen book. The methodical Krall measured each band, cataloguing each individual chunk of text, and forming the columns for the first time. Realizing the enormity of the task, Krall consulted his library, and his colleagues. He realized that the Egyptian context of the find was a red herring: these were the words of an Etruscan writer. Over a century later, the linen strips look discoloured. Yet the script upon them is still clear to see, arranged in twelve columns running from right to left. The first three columns are poorly preserved and almost impossible to read, but the rest are legible, if incomplete.

It is at this point that we need to return to the second major issue with Etruscan writing. The mummy is unwrapped, the script is acknowledged as Etruscan, everything is ready: what does this unique text say? What does the only known surviving Etruscan linen book actually tell us? The answer is, painfully little – because we still do not understand Etruscan as a language. Yes, we can read the letters, familiar from Greek and Phoenician sources, and the foundation for Latin script. Indeed, 21 out of 26 letters in the Latin alphabet have Etruscan origins. But we do not understand all the words that are formed. It is the opposite problem to the classical

Bucchero vase in the shape of a cockerel inscribed with the letters of the Etruscan alphabet: perhaps an inkwell?

example of ancient linguistic code breaking: the translation of Egyptian hieroglyphics. In that case, the issue was that the text was unreadable, but understandable. Unfortunately, as far as we know, Etruscan as a language is almost totally isolated. It is not part of the dominant Indo-European language family which is spoken all over Europe and Asia. The shared roots of languages as far apart as Sanskrit and English are visible in tables of cognates, closely related words for the same object or person. For example, here are seven different Indo-European languages, and their words for 'mother' and 'water':[6]

LANGUAGE	MOTHER	WATER
(Old) English	Modor	Water
Latin	Mater	Aqua
Classical Attic Greek	Meter	Hydor
Sanskrit	Matar	Apa
Old Persian	Matar	Aoda
Lithuanian	Moteris	Vanduo
Albanian	Moter	Uje

The Etruscan word for 'mother', by contrast, seems to have been 'ati'. The Etruscan word for water seems likely to have been 'thi'. Both are very different in terms of their sound and composition from their Indo-European counterparts. There are languages with similarities: scholars have suggested that Lemnian, a dialect spoken only on the island of Lemnos, might have developed from the language of Etruscan-speaking traders who settled there. There is also a relationship with Raetic, a tongue spoken in parts of Switzerland and Austria. The two languages seem to share fundamental grammatical structures. Roman sources link these people with the Etruscans, but it is a chicken-and-egg situation: did the Raetians pick up Etruscan from contact with traders in northern Italy, or did the two people share a common origin? Even the inscriptions from Lemnian and Raetic do not help much in the quest to understand Etruscan. There are not enough examples to settle the issue of whether the three tongues are linked to one another in what has been termed the Tyrrhenian language family.[7] Other, more problematic, connections have been made, with some scholars looking to Anatolia, others to the Near East and still others to Hungary. The latter idea, sparked in the nineteenth century, has been systematically disproven, but popped up once again in 2003. A link to Semitic languages was also popular during the Victorian era, but attempts to prove a connection failed.[8] The Anatolian theory is the most persistent, and the concept of a connection between Etruscan and Luwian (the language probably spoken in the city we know as Troy) lingers.[9] Even into the 1960s, new language links were proposed and disproven: Albanian as Etruscan, in spite of its Indo-European status?[10]

The problem with these ideas was their shared reliance on one method of translation, known as the etymological method. When languages are related to one another, as demonstrated in the table above, there are clear links in their words and their grammatical structure. However, it is easy to see connections that do not exist. Single-word similarities exist almost everywhere: for example, the word for bone in Japanese is coincidentally *hone*, pronounced bone. One nineteenth-century scholar, Wilhelm Paul Corssen (1820–1875), dedicated his career to proving a link between Etruscan and Latin beyond later loanwords using this method. He died shortly after a devastating critique of his work demonstrated the circular nature of this kind of argument: a link exists, therefore these words are similar; these words are similar, therefore a link exists. This technique, of cherry-picking words that sound a bit like something else, still crops up. However, it has largely been replaced, not by a single method, but by three different approaches that have attacked the Etruscan language from all angles.

This way of working is termed the 'combinatory' method, using every possible clue, and building these blocks together to decipher the broad strokes of the Etruscan language. The first aspect of this approach is to look at letters, words and structures, looking for the way that grammar shapes a language. For example, does the ending of a word shift in different contexts? Could it be plural, or possessive? How about prefixes – are there standard beginnings to words? Once these repetitive little add-ons are removed, you are left with a root word. For example, the word 'use': we can have useful, usefully, used, using, user and misuse. In this case, the three-letter construction 'use' unites all these different words and they form a family. Or we can look at suffixes – for example, we might see useful, faithful, regretful, mournful and so on. An Etruscan example is '*qutum*', meaning 'jug'. We also find '*qutumuza*', which seems to mean 'little jug'.[11] Now, if we see 'za' elsewhere, we are halfway to breaking into the word – something is little.

The first task of the combinatory method can only get you so far in a world of limited inscriptions. The next wave of attack is to look at the word differently. Instead of stripping it down to its parts, place it back into the context of the sentence in which it is being used, and into the corpus of Etruscan inscriptions. So, on a bucchero vase from Veii, we have the phrase '*mini alice velthur*'.[12] Velthur, we know, is a personal name. So what would a person called Velthur have been doing with a bucchero vessel to want it inscribed with his name? Could it be that Velthur was the potter? The other words in the sentence, found on other inscriptions, make this unlikely. The 'ali' preface seems to designate a gift, the act of giving. It appears in other contexts with personal names, given distinctive endings. The adaptation of a name suggests a variance in case: perhaps the genitive case that expresses possession, or, more likely in this instance, the dative case, indicating that the person named is receiving something. But Velthur is unchanged. So Velthur is not receiving anything. What could he be doing instead, relating to a gift? Velthur is the giver. And 'mini'? 'Mi' is a pronoun which appears in a large range of inscriptions, but here it has a changed ending. Just as with the names, the change to a familiar pronoun suggests a case is at play. In the context of this example, the case is accusative, making it clear that this is the object affected by the verb 'alice'. So, putting it all together, we have: '*Mini alice velthur*' – 'Velthur gave me'.

The final stage is to step out of the world of language and go back to the archaeology. This is perhaps the oldest method in the search for the Etruscan language. A friar, Annio da Viterbo, claimed in the fifteenth century that he could entirely translate Etruscan. In fact, he put together a book devoted to lost Etruscan manuscripts that he had found and translated.[13] A native of Viterbo, it was suspiciously convenient that according to these miraculously recovered documents, this city was the ancient seat of power in central Italy. It was also supposedly the greatest religious centre and the most important influence on Rome. Annio's texts were, unsurprisingly, utter forgeries. When he stretched himself to fabricating texts by more famous Roman authors, the intelligentsia of Renaissance Italy began asking questions. Even so, it would not be until 1565 that his discoveries were exposed as fakes. In a neat twist, his unmasking came as part of a later piece of political appropriation of archaeology: an appeal to Annio as part of a Medici marriage contract drew the attention of an anti-Medici scholar, who went for the jugular.[14] Once it was clear that Annio had made a basic mistake regarding the foundation of Florence, the rest of his work was instantly suspect.

Fortunately, in the intervening centuries, archaeological investigation of the Etruscan language has become more reputable. From the early twentieth century, more and more contextual information for inscribed finds (the places they came from, the objects they were found with) has been preserved to provide an insight into the way texts were being used in Etruscan society. This gives background to words and phrases, putting them into place linguistically. Excavations in the twentieth and twenty-first centuries have been revealing new Etruscan inscriptions on a regular basis. In 1964 a particularly astounding object was uncovered. Excavators in the ancient port of Cerveteri, known as Pyrgi, carefully removed three golden tablets, all of which were covered in writing.[15] There was a full archaeological context for the find, which gave a significant hint as to the purpose of the plaques, but the major clue was the presence of nail holes: they were a proclamation, attached to the walls of the port's sanctuary complex.

Knowing the context of the Pyrgi tablets was a big step towards translating this complex document – one of the oldest extended Etruscan texts, dating back to around 500 BCE. What do public service announcements in busy international transport hubs need to be able to work? They need to be multilingual. So it proved: the Pyrgi text was written in Phoenician and Etruscan, presumably sending the same message in the two most commonly spoken languages through the alleys of the port. Indeed, Phoenician inscriptions have been found on ceramic fragments from Pyrgi too. Helpfully, as a Semitic language related to Hebrew, Phoenician

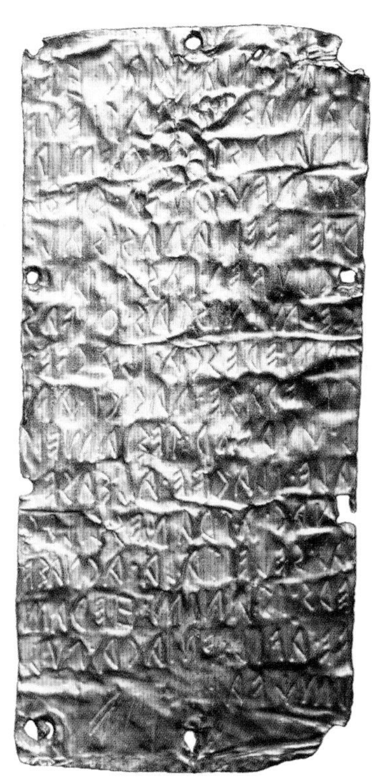

The golden Pyrgi tablets, which bear Etruscan and Phoenician script, *c*. 500 BCE.

can be read.[16] Therefore, the Phoenician inscription can be usefully compared to the Etruscan one, and the two are very similar. They both record the dedication of a small shrine to the goddess Uni, who in both inscriptions is referred to by her Eastern name, Astarte, in addition to her Etruscan one. The man who built the new shrine, who is named *thefarie velianas* in the Etruscan text, and *tbry wlns* in the Phoenician (and who can be Latinized into Tiberias Velianas), was determined that everybody knew how generous he was, and how devoted to Uni/Astarte he was. So he produced what must be some of the flashiest posters in history, proclaiming that as the goddess' favourite he was 'in the palm of her hand'.[17]

The Pyrgi tablets provide a series of insights into life in this Etruscan port. First, that politicians, then as now, enjoy self-promotion; Thefarie Velianas is described as a *zilath,* an Etruscan magistrate, but he was clearly a highly successful one in his third yearly term. Second, that the divine right to rule was an asset for this powerful ruler and carried weight with his public.[18] Third, and most importantly, that the best way to reach a large proportion of this public was to write down and display words. Not pictures. Words. The implication of the Pyrgi texts is that at the time they were pinned up on the wall, there was an expectation that they would be read. Not just by priests or the wealthy, but by people going about their business – foreign traders and Etruscan merchant families, middling folks caught by the flash of gold. By writing down the details of his extravagant gift, and the gratitude of the goddess, Thefarie Velianas was taking advantage of a remarkable level of literacy among the people he ruled over. Etruscan people were reading and writing far beyond the truncated inscriptions they left on tomb furniture. Nor should this be a surprise: from the

Burial urn of Aulus Petronius, named in its Etruscan inscription, 2nd century.

eighth century, even ordinary objects were inscribed with letters and names. Thefarie Velianas was sure that the best way to publicize his magistracy and relationship with the goddess was to write about it.

In Pyrgi in 500 BCE, we can see a society in which words matter, and in which people are expected to be able to read. The same holds true for the intended readership of the Zagreb texts, inked onto their linen pages at least two hundred years later.[19] Over these two centuries, deep and sweeping changes took place that marked the beginning of the end for Etruscan culture. The rot had already set in by 474 BCE, when Etruscan control of Campania wobbled and collapsed in the wake of the Battle of Cumae, when Greek settlers trounced an Etruscan naval force.[20] Trade routes were disrupted, the wealth of Etruria threatened. Then, in the early fourth century BCE, an upstart southern city began to look northward and threaten its neighbours: Rome.[21] Steadily, the Etruscan language was effaced by the tongue of its southern rival. Latin and Etruscan vied for popularity; the confused situation of many families can be seen in their funerary inscriptions. No longer content with solely Etruscan names above a door, the individual burial urns of a number of wealthy families now carried bilingual inscriptions. By the time the author of the Zagreb texts was writing, Etruscan as a living language was doomed. The romantic image of an Etruscan text smuggled into Egyptian exile seems unlikely; rather, the Zagreb mummy's recycling of a once-treasured linen book demonstrates the irrelevance of the language. Slowly, through a thousand such degradations, Etruscan begins to ebb away from the archaeological record.

Occasional revivals of interest did occur: the Roman emperor Claudius is one of the last recorded Etruscan speakers, making his first marriage into an Etruscan family. The later infidelity of his wife, Plautia Urgulanilla, did not seem to dampen his curiosity about Etruscan culture.[22] Claudius was particularly interested in the religion of the Etruscans, notably their supposed skill at reading the future.[23] It was this connection of the Etruscan language with the occult that finally sealed its fate. The Etruscan texts in libraries and archives would not survive the onslaught of a new religion, which

Gold aureus of Claudius: the emperor was fascinated by Etruscan culture.

actively competed with Etruscan belief, as the following chapter exposes. Between the destruction wrought by zealous Christians and the inevitable collateral damage, the few linen books that had survived the first fall of Etruria (to Rome) vanished.

Between the universally readable glory days of the Pyrgi tablets and the mistaken ascription of the Zagreb texts lies 2,400 years. Yet through the efforts of scholars making use of the combinatory method, pulling together linguistic evidence and archaeological information, the scraps of writing on the linen bandages can be read. The book seems to have been a guide to the religious festivals that defined the Etruscan year. As such, it provides snippets of detailed insight into the organization of the Etruscan religious calendar. One of the translated segments refers to a specific date: 26 September. On this day, gifts must be given to the sea god, Nethyns/Neptune. These gifts are also specified – they should be offerings of wine. The book would have ordered the lives of an Etruscan community, marking the passage of the seasons, laying out the requirements of the gods to secure health, wealth and long life.[24]

Writing retains this same power: to thrill and to command. In a digital world dictated by the keyboard, we are more reliant than ever before on the written word. Communication by phone and by computer is reliant on text. We have a thousand libraries at our fingertips, access to digital books and online videos that can transport us into new worlds. The story of the Etruscan language, its disappearance and its partial recovery, remains relevant in this new world of text. Languages are dying all the time, preserved only in digital archives, which are just as vulnerable as linen texts. Any language can vanish, while words fall out of usage and vanish from the vernacular. Looking into the future, is the digital realm a safe storage place for our literature and our cultural identity? Are paper books, still cherished for their physicality, likely to be the only repositories of the written word that survive?

More positively, technological advances will hopefully advance the parlour game of linguistics. Computer simulations can test and scan through texts, pulling out and comparing words from multiple ancient documents.[25] The work of examining the entire corpus of Etruscan literature in search of a single word could be drastically reduced, and with speed may come breakthroughs. In the archaeological world, new discoveries are happening all the time. In the late 1990s, one of the longest known Etruscan inscriptions, a series of bronze tablets, was handed in to the police station in the Tuscan hilltown of Cortona.[26] Another Zagreb text, another linen book, may have survived out there somewhere. Little by little, more evidence for the Etruscan language is flowing in, and new technologies are developing to make the most of it. Perhaps this central component of the Etruscan legend, the untranslatable tongue, may crumble yet.

TEN

LISTENING TO LIVERS

The religious identity of the Etruscan people is stuck fast to their reputation, so much so that it is perhaps the central feature in our modern vision of them. The idea of the Etruscans as mysterious, while having strong roots in the problems of the Etruscan language and the lack of a clear narrative for Etruscan origins, is closely entwined with the religious beliefs of these people. This is perplexing. How much can we really know about what people believed 2,500 years ago? One's religious belief, one's faith in the efficacy of the rituals that define social and spiritual life, is an intensely personal phenomenon. The archaeology and history can provide a rough idea of what could have been happening behind the closed eyes of the Etruscan supplicant. The archaeology provides the props and gadgets, the bells and whistles of faith. The historical texts give the views of outsiders, including proponents of competitor religions from late antiquity, notably a persistent new belief system focused on a Judean prophet. The absolute reality of belief is unknown and unknowable from the outset.

That said, religious artefacts are as close as we can get to seeing belief made real. Someone, somewhere, invested their time and resources in creating a thing that would enable their faith. This chapter's central object is one of these. It creates belief by its very presence, providing its users with a guide to the workings of the Etruscan religious universe. It is a late survivor from the Etruscan world, a century younger than the Zagreb mummy wrappings, themselves only scribbled after the end of Etruscan dominance in Italy.[1] It is evidence for the persistence of Etruscan beliefs, their strength and their continuity. It is one of the most important Etruscan artefacts ever excavated. And it is just 12.6 cm long. This little scrap of bronze was found in a field in late September 1877, far from the hills of Tuscany, and still further north than the ravines of Marzabotto.[2] The field lay on the flat, fertile valley of the River Trebbia, oozing northwards towards northern Italy's major river, the great Po, in the breadbasket of Italy. In 1877 this was a relatively comfortable, affluent area, free from the poverty that made life elsewhere a struggle.

This distinction is important. That such a discovery was handed in speaks volumes of the ploughman who found it. That he spotted such a tiny speck of green bronze in front of the horse-drawn plough, and recognized its importance, was a chain of events that might not have happened elsewhere. Once the dirt of the field was removed, the queer shape of the little bronze bulge was visible. It had strange lumps and bumps on its flat surface. On the right, there was an odd pattern of lines fanning out from a central point; on the left there was a set of inscribed lines that made up a pattern which looked like brickwork. Around the edge was a border, carefully defined and following the contours of its defined edge, itself only slightly degraded by its centuries in the soil. After the little bronze

The famous Piacenza Liver, found in a ploughed field and evidence for the continued teaching of Etruscan religious skills.

was cleaned up, it could be seen that it was covered in inscriptions, with each area sketched out and labelled with letters. In total, there were sixteen named segments running around the outer rim and a further 24 sections on the interior, all squashed onto this small object. On its bottom face two further words were inscribed. Whatever this object was, it was designed to be read, and examined closely. The strange shape and the weird lumps and bumps suddenly began to make sense in the context of historical texts: this was a life-sized model of a sheep's liver.

The Piacenza Liver, as this little artefact has become known (which can be seen in the Palazzo Farnese museum in Piacenza), is evidence of the longevity and power of one of humanity's greatest interests: the prediction of the future. Its specific form was akin to far older objects from other, more ancient, cultures. A similar clay example survives from the great city of Babylon.[3] Made about 1,400 years earlier, this liver, too, is covered with inscriptions, in cuneiform script. Like the Piacenza Liver, it shows the gall bladder, caudate lobe and vena cava: all features that occur in the liver of a real sheep. Ironically, we have more information about the context of use for the Bronze Age Babylonian liver than we do the example from Piacenza. Texts survive outlining a special priest, known as a *baru*, who would use his knowledge of livers to assist with major decisions of state.[4] The *baru*, a man of impeccable family who lived a pure life, would be the person to interpret the will of the gods to advise the king.

Thirty-six individual inscribed livers have also been uncovered from the great citadel of Hattusa, capital of the Hittite Empire, which ruled over Turkey in the middle of the second millennium BCE.[5] As a result of this seemingly shared interest in animal livers, the later Piacenza Liver was very quickly co-opted into the argument for Etruscan origins. By 1901, only a generation after its discovery, it was adopted by a German scholar, Ludwig Stieda (1837–1918), as evidence for the shared relationship between Turkey and Etruria.[6] However, there is a distinctively Etruscan story of the introduction of the practice of reading animal entrails, or hepatoscopy, that defies Stieda's interpretation of this evidence. It survives in patches of Roman texts, which reference a lost Etruscan book: the *Libri*

Tagetici.[7] Cicero provides one version of the tale, and Ovid another.[8] The two versions are similar enough to suggest a well-known myth with important narrative details.

The story starts with another ploughed field, this time in the Etruscan heartland near Tarquinia. A ploughman stumbled on a crater in his path. Laying in the hole was a little boy with the face of an old man. The ploughman cried out, and a crowd gathered. The child spoke to the people, who were overwhelmed by his wisdom. He first revealed his name, Tarchnes, adapted in Latin to Tages.[9] He then showed the assembled crowd how to read the will of the gods, and the events of the future, through the signs of birds flying in the heavens, and in the entrails of beasts. He also shared with the people his knowledge of the underworld, and the dangers of death. The literate among the congregation dashed home to commit to paper what they had heard – the foundations for the first Etruscan holy books.

The fable references the knowledge bestowed by Tages as arising from Italian soil. There are no mysterious arrivals from across the seas who bring power with them – no sign of Eastern origins. His revelations come first to a poor ploughman. It is not a tale which bestows power to a particular family, individual, ruling house or caste. There are no gods directly involved in the transaction; the child-prophet Tages speaks of them but not for them. The great prophet takes the form of a child, and it is through this weak physical vessel that the knowledge of the gods comes to the people. The literacy of the people suggests that this tale dates to the eighth century BCE at the earliest, although the earliest representation of the Tages myth is on a third-century mirror.[10] In a fascinating twist, excavations of a temple at Tarquinia's Pian di Civita have revealed that within its foundations was placed the body of a child with epilepsy, perhaps given to strange visions while in the throes of fits.[11] Whether or not this sad little body represents a perceived heir of Tages, or has a closer link to the legend, it emphasizes the strength, longevity and importance of this myth to the Etruscan people.

The story of Tages is not unique. Other Etruscan prophets appeared to the people, with different regions of Etruria preferring their own local links to the divine, with their own magical specialities. Further north, in Chiusi, it was a young woman who revealed a different method for telling the future. Less survives of her story, but she is named as Vegoia in later Roman sources, and her Etruscan name was probably Vecu.[12] Unlike Tages, we know little of her emergence as a prophetess, or which signs she correctly interpreted to convince the populace of her knowledge. The texts do give a hint: she is supposed to have been an expert in the reading of lightning in the skies, and the flight of birds overhead. Vegoia is also attributed with a practical skill that must have seemed like magic: she could control water, bringing the life-giving liquid to the thirsty people. This is a tiny scrap of a clue to the date of her existence: cuniculi, or rock-cut drainage channels, are tricky to date but seem to have been created from the sixth century onwards.[13] Another hint at a chronological setting for this story comes from the dividing of the sky into different sections, an act which allowed Vegoia to dictate the units of measurement used by her people. The Etruscan word *naper* refers to a specific distance, perhaps the length of a particular kind of rope, while buildings seem to adhere to a measurement of 27 cm – one 'Italic foot'. This measurement is attested to from the sixth century BCE.[14] The practical sound of this knowledge belies its magic: to be able to create regular and safe buildings, with beautiful proportions pleasing to the eye. The skills attributed to Vegoia are bound up in the everyday. They emphasize the centrality of religious belief to Etruscan life, down to the digging of a channel in a remote field. Just as in the tale of Tages, even the poor may experience the wonders of the gods, as revealed by the talents of a prophetess.

The Piacenza Liver bears traces of the lost knowledge imparted by these prophet figures. The sixteen segments around the outside adhere to the divisions of the sky that the Roman author Pliny describes the Etruscans as using in their analyses of lightning and birds.[15] That the same methods could be used for the reading of livers suggests an element of shared practice. There are objects from across Etruria showing the same image – a fortune-teller standing with their weight on one leg, the other raised and leaning on a rock.[16] In their left hands, the figures hold a liver. In front of them is usually depicted a table, or an altar, on which other pieces of the

Libation bowl for religious use, made in Orvieto, *c.* 250–200 BCE.

dead animal are laid. The pose seems to be important: suspended between heaven and earth, in the right place to read the will of the gods. The majority of these images show male soothsayers, but inscriptions describe women as occupying important religious roles, even if they are more rarely depicted on the job.[17]

All these images are late in date, and they correlate beautifully with the later Roman texts. However, this is only a tiny snapshot of a vast period of time during which Etruscan people's beliefs were changing. Trying to trace the stories of the prophets back in time is problematic, even with the tempting snippets of archaeological evidence that might back up these tales. The archaeology suggests a different focus for belief, based not on prophets and fortune-telling, but on a cast of divinities able to bestow their especial favour. The earliest temples, like the Ara della Regina in

Tarquinia (which developed and grew steadily between the eighth and seventh centuries BCE) and Portonaccio in Veii (dating back to around the middle of the sixth century BCE), began their existence as straightforward shrines, buildings with three distinct sections, in addition to an open porch-like area.[18] This three-fold structure fits well with the concept of tripartite ritual, in which people shift through three distinct phases of being. We can see this kind of ritual retained in the modern ceremonies that mark shifts in the life course: from baptism to graduation to burial. There is a before, a during and an after. The most important moment is the point at which a change in state takes place, the moment of becoming. In encounters with the divine, this is the moment at which the god (or gods) are working on or with the supplicant. In the physical remains of the Etruscan temple we can envision people moving from normal life to encounters with the gods, and then returning to their everyday existence.

One of the greatest forms of evidence for the shape and structure of these encounters themselves are the remains of items deposited in and around these religious buildings. At the Pian di Civita, Tarquinia, in addition to the remains of the central child, there are burials of infants with cranial deformations. Here, too, is the remains of a channel leading to a rock chasm, which seems to have been used for the choreographed disposal of liquids: perhaps blood from animal sacrifices, more probably wine. There are also two clearly planned and carefully laid out incidents of destruction. In one pit by the entranceway, dated to the early seventh century BCE, an axe, shield and curved trumpet were placed. All three items were deliberately broken, ensuring that they could never be recovered and reused. In another nearby pit, a full dining set of ten plates and two cups was smashed to pieces and buried. This activity of giving an object irretrievably to a divinity, in hope of receiving a gift in return, seems to have been a central practice in this early form of Etruscan religious practice, in common with other European Bronze and Iron Age communities.[19]

Parts of temple buildings, too, may form part of this tradition, recycled as a cult object after redevelopment. The most impressive example of this is at the site of Poggio Colla, near Florence.[20] Here, the remnants of the earliest temple on the site were literally turned upside down when the second phase of development began. A large sandstone block was placed over a rock fissure, which led to a chamber below ground, designed to block access to what had perhaps been the original seat of ritual power at the site. To emphasize the strangeness of the block's new home, it was laid out the wrong way up. To seal the deal, a gold ring and a piece of gold wire were placed next to the great block, before the entirety of this thoughtfully designed collection of objects was buried. In another area, a cylindrical piece of sandstone, perhaps a small altar or part of a column, was also turned on its head.[21] The time and effort that went into planning and executing these deposits is a testament to the strength of Etruscan belief.

These grand gestures naturally steal the spotlight, but smaller deposits were more common, and provide some of the best evidence for the identities of the divinity to whom they were given.[22] Inscriptions mark out the name of the god, with different levels of detail. Pottery vessels may simply be scrawled with a two-word statement of dedication: 'mi uni'. Longer inscriptions might provide the identity of the giver. Sadly, there are few hints as to their motive. One exception is votive offerings made of clay or bronze in the shape of body parts, presumably malfunctioning internal organs, genitals and limbs.[23] But by looking at the gods to whom such objects were dedicated, we can see regional preferences – particular divinities worshipped in certain places. For example, the Belvedere temple at Orvieto, one of the best-preserved Etruscan temples that you can visit today, seems to have been sacred to the god Tinia.[24] At Pyrgi, and perhaps at the Ara della Regina in Tarquinia, the principal deity may have been the goddess Uni.[25] At Veii, the Portonaccio temple was dedicated to the goddess Menrva, while another temple just outside the city walls was dedicated to the god Aplu.[26] The latter two names are very close to the Roman and Greek names for these divinities, Minerva and Apollo respectively.

From depictions and their accompanying labels, it seems that the majority of the Etruscan pantheon had at least a passing resemblance to the gods of Olympus and their later Roman equivalents.[27]

Tinia, the Etruscan sky and thunder god, at first glance equates neatly to Zeus, while Aita, the ruler of the underworld, finds a parallel in Hades. There are deities with similar concerns, perhaps reflecting the major features of life in the ancient world, the serious concerns of worshippers. With trade and contact between the Greek and Etruscan worlds flourishing, the representation of shared deities could have been an important point of reference between the two cultures. However, it is a mistake to assume that the Etruscan gods had the same attributes and the same responsibilities as their counterparts in Greece. There seem to have been distinct differences between the role of Athena and that of Menrva; the latter did not have the same dedication to craftwork, and instead seems to have been connected with child rearing, and potentially with healing powers.[28] Similarly, the aforementioned Tinia is often represented as a beardless youth, instead of the burly bearded Zeus.[29]

Older trading relationships, and closer allies, also influenced the divine line-up of the Etruscan heavens. The Pyrgi texts present a vision in which the Etruscan goddess Uni (often compared to Hera as prime female deity, and whose name is surely linked to the Roman Juno) could be equated with the Near Eastern goddess Astarte. The latter, with her links to the Babylonian goddess Ishtar, was one of the most popular female deities of the ancient world, worshipped across a vast area. Unlike Hera, who was tied to wifedom and her philandering husband, Astarte's attributes are an intoxicating mixture of sexuality and death. In the *Epic of Gilgamesh*, her actions cause the death of the hero's best friend, Enkidu.[30] She is immensely, independently, powerful, and is represented as such. It is these Near Eastern images that seem to have informed depictions of the Etruscan goddess Uni. In one of the most famous Near Eastern examples, now in the British Museum, Astarte stands proudly nude between two owls, ferocious hunters of the night. Other scenes show her with deadly big cats.[31]

This representative trope is so widespread it has its own terminology: the goddess in this aspect is known as the Potnia Theron, or the Mistress of Animals.[32] This representative style, of the winged woman between two felines, is widespread in Etruria: it pops up on pottery, and is central to the design of the decorative terracottas at Poggio Civitate.[33] This winged female deity is also shown as literally the power behind the throne on ceramics from Chiusi, and more speculatively could be the vision of Uni worshipped at Tarquinia. In Greece, this goddess became a number of deities, with aspects of the original Mistress of Animals appearing in the attributes of Artemis, Hera, Athena and Aphrodite. In Etruria, Uni seems to have retained a closer connection to her Near Eastern cousins. It was not until the great shift in Etruscan religion in the early fourth century that this goddess's grip on the Etruscan ritual

Bucchero chalice with female heads, perhaps related to the Potnia Theron, or the 'Mistress of Animals'.

imagination began to falter, and representations of an alternative love-goddess, Turan/Aphrodite, began to surge in popularity.

This change is one aspect of the so-called watershed of Etruscan religion, a tumultuous change that looks to have taken place in the fourth century BCE.[34] It marks the rise of prophets and prophecy as key features of Etruscan ritual practice. In spite of this shift in the focus of belief, the gods did not suddenly disappear from people's lives. Indeed, the sixteen segments around the exterior of the Piacenza Liver are each labelled with the name of a divinity. They include Tinia, Uni, Nethuns (Neptune) and Fufluns (Dionysus). On the interior segments, a further gang of gods and heroes are named, this time including Hercle/Herakles, Leda, Mars and Turan/Aphrodite. It is difficult to ascertain whether the Piacenza Liver represents an ancient tradition, recording the continued belief in gods as part of a practice of prophecy, or whether these older deities were latterly co-opted into the new focus of belief that emerged at this point. However, it is the practice itself, the reading of the future, that would be remembered as the central force of Etruscan religion.

The continued importance of gods and heroes poses a question: why introduce prophets and prophecy at all? Why did this happen? It seems too simplistic to accept a purely historical explanation for this key change in Etruscan religious behaviour. Prophets become important when people are dissatisfied with the answers they are receiving from deities; people become frustrated with deities when their luck seems to run steadily downhill. Another shift in Etruscan religious belief might be visible in the emergence of images of death demons, monstrous creatures who remake the underworld as a terrifying place filled with danger. In these changes, we can see a newly pessimistic society, living off past glories and fearful about the future, placing its trust in prophets and picking apart animal entrails to gain some sense of security in an uncertain world – perhaps a familiar vision? In an uncertain world, those who claim foreknowledge of impending disaster have a kind of glamour that inevitably gains a following: as in modern Doomsday cults, perhaps so in the political turmoil of an Etruria overrun by Rome.

The uncanny accuracy of Etruscan soothsayers was a source of endless fascination to the newly powerful Romans: supposedly, the sage who advised Julius Caesar to 'Beware the Ides of March' was an Etruscan priest called Spurinna.[35] That Etruscan religious ideas survived the overthrow of the culture that produced them is in itself intriguing. While Roman society prided itself on its gluttonous incorporation of alien belief systems, and its relative tolerance towards different religions, it seems strange that Etruscan knowledge remained so revered for such a long period of time. Perhaps this was because the Roman practice of borrowing Etruscan ritual practices made the assimilation of the two religions a smooth one, in which Etruscan divination techniques acquired the name 'disciplina', giving them a scientific status that acknowledged Etruscan expertise in this area. Indeed, Roman legions and even the emperor himself had a specific haruspex (a priest with a particular interest in foretelling), emphasizing the integration of Etruscan religion into the apparatus of the Roman state.[36]

Etruscan religion and Etruscan religious science did not, however, survive the onslaught of a later prophet and his believers. Christianity shared several key features with Etruscan religion – notably the worship of a prophet who comes into the world as a child. This was probably enough for Christians to view Etruscan religious practice as a distinct threat.[37] The Christian author Tertullian, writing in the second century CE, names several Etruscan sages on his hit lists of religious fraudsters and con artists.[38] The threat posed by Etruscan beliefs to Christians was also a literal one: it was the imperial haruspex, heir to the *Etrusca disciplina* – the texts recording the words of the prophet Tages, which were continually updated and modified throughout the Roman period – who was charged with spurring on the Emperor Diocletian to his persecution of Christians in the third century CE.[39] In this climate of mutual disdain and fear, what could be perceived as a struggle for hearts and minds became very much a battle to the death. Slowly and inevitably, after the conversion of the Emperor Constantine to Christianity, Etruscan belief lost its grip on the apparatus of the Roman state, and the number of believers dwindled.

The fraught relationship between Etruscan and Christian religion would colour the perception of the Etruscans throughout the Middle Ages. Pagan rituals dripping with literal blood created a vision of a terrifying cult, using devilish techniques to rule by fear. The combination of terror and fascination created in this period is one of the roots of the modern idea of the 'mysterious' Etruscan, a figure who can read the future but is powerless to prevent his or her own destruction. Yet there are hints of Etruscan heritage that pop up regularly in medieval art, suggesting a representative tradition that stubbornly survived the cultural upheavals of the Migration Age. Even the most holy of Christian icons can be seen to have Etruscan elements: the Etruscan representation of death demons as winged humans deeply influenced the depiction of later angels. Scenes of Uni/Hera breastfeeding the baby Ercle/Heracles shifted into images of the Virgin and Child, with bare-breasted Marian iconography popular in medieval Italy as a result.[40]

In our modern world, faith and belief are continuously shifting. In some quarters, religious belief has been almost entirely supplanted by science – the victory of the Roman idea of *disciplina*: education, training, knowledge and order. In other areas of the world, the intensity and conviction that religion inspires leads to violence and suffering. World religions struggle with the battle between peaceful acceptance of the truth and bringing that truth to others, whether they want to hear it or not. Even sects that preach non-violence are susceptible to fanaticism – and that includes non-believers. Doomsday groups prepare for the end of the world, whether in strange cultic compounds or by casually filling cellars with tins against a scientifically brewed nuclear holocaust or climatic disaster. We are once again looking to the skies for ways to read the future, scanning atmospheric conditions for evidence that the planet itself is changing. The Etruscan science of fortune-telling is alive and well, whether through interpreting the words of latter prophets with reference to current affairs or through the use of data to analyse the events that structure our modern lives. From spotting a housing market crash to triggering tsunami early warning systems, we are relying ever more intensely on a new form of haruspicy to replace the religions that no longer fit with a world filled with knowledge and relative certainty. The twentieth century marked a change in belief which mirrors that of the fourth-century seismic shift in Etruscan religion. Instead of listening to livers, we are now agog for 24-hour news. In a world dissatisfied with gods, we are turning to a new kind of prophet – not sprung out of the ploughsoil but from the laboratory.

ELEVEN

Facing Oblivion

There is really only one certainty in life: everything ends. Death comes for everyone, whether after a century of loose living or an unlucky car accident, years of invalidism or a sudden heart attack. The end result is the same: a person who once walked and talked, loved and was loved, vanishes. In the privileged bubble of twenty-first-century medicine, we are fortunate to rarely encounter death at first hand. It is there, of course, just around the corner, happening to other people, making headlines. The corpse itself is removed, sanitized, cleaned, made up, all by professionals who make death their business. Once disposed of, it is permanently cast aside, dropping into the heat of the crematorium behind the grim curtains of a chapel of rest, or efficiently shovelled over with dirt. As a result of these two phenomena – the relative rareness of our experiences with death and the physical alienation of the dead from the living – we are deeply uncomfortable with this inevitable prospect. What happens when we die? For all the advances of science, we still don't know, and are unlikely to.

The objects in this book have been intimately connected with Etruscan people's preparedness for the end of life. In the survival of so many tombs and the destruction of so many settlements, a quirk of fate has given the Etruscans a morbid reputation. The ingredients of the myth of the mysterious Etruscan include their perceived lack of a coherent origin, their untranslatable language, their interest and expertise in predicting the future, their political annihilation

Elaborate wine jug: solace at a time of familial and political upheaval?

at the hands of their Roman neighbours. All these different facets have come together into the concept of an unknowable people. The final flourish is in the perceived Etruscan obsession with death. That a society could invest so heavily in tombs, their decoration and their furnishings, sets it at a great distance from our own world in which the fact of our own impending death is feared and deliberately forgotten. Yet both cultures were, and are, attempting to do the same thing, through different means: the Etruscan preparation for death had the same function as our deliberate exclusion of it; both are coping mechanisms.

Sarteano is a sleepy little Tuscan town. It doesn't have hordes of visitors thronging through the streets each summer. But it is important. It lies at around the midpoint of a journey between the two major valleys of this area, in which the Chiana and the Orcia rivers flow inexorably southward. Only a few miles away to the west are the steep slopes and escarpments of Chiusi and Montepulciano. On the other side of town, once you head out of the centre on a dusty track, you can look back eastwards towards the latter valley, crowned by the highest point in Tuscany, Monte Amiata. Etruscan tombs were known to be dotted about the countryside, and the town's small museum had a respectable number of finds from the period. It was largely dismissed as a little rural settlement on the road from Chiusi to the rich farmland of the Val d'Orcia and the coast, with possible links to a further Etruscan centre to the

Set of bronze plates from a burial, evidence of conspicuous consumption: the deliberate disposal of wealth in the grave.

south: Cetona.[1] In 2003, however, one necropolis, on the south-eastern side of town, proved that this little town still had the ability to surprise the archaeological community.

Excavations had restarted in the Pianacce necropolis in the year 2000. The first formal digging had begun in the mid-1950s.[2] That first dig had revealed a massive tumulus, with an entrance corridor that measured 30 metres from end to end. Researchers felt that there was more to be found, and they were right. In 2003 archaeologists revealed one of the most remarkable survivals from the Etruscan world, uncovering a burial chamber.[3] When they entered, they did not see the 'wonderful things' that archaeological cliché might have led them to expect. Instead, they encountered a nightmarish vision. On every wall were brightly painted frescoes, but their subjects were terrifying. A red-headed figure swathed in a vivid red robe whips on four ghostly white horses, urging them to a dangerously fast gallop as they chase after a smaller man running for his life. On closer inspection, you can see that the horses have the paws and claws of lions, and a big cat's curved tail. Two men gravely look into each other's eyes, with the younger reaching up to touch the elder's stubbled chin. To their right, a triple-headed serpent rears. On the back wall are sea monsters, and stood in front of them is a badly damaged sarcophagus.[4]

The entire effect of the tomb is unsettling. It's possible to visit, on Saturday mornings, alongside a member of the museum staff.[5] As you travel down the corridor towards the doorway, the temperature steadily drops. The atmosphere becomes damp, the air heavy. The colours of the tomb are still vivid, thanks to the carefully controlled visitor numbers and the vigilance of curators. This is what the more famous examples further south must once have looked like to the Etruscan families placing their loved ones inside. Unfortunately, you are following the path taken by medieval tomb robbers, who reused the burial place and recycled the majority of the objects this family vault once contained. Some items remained and are now safe in Sarteano's museum. These included a series of opaque glass gaming pieces and a series of ceramics, the majority used for the service of food and wine, but also one used as a perfume vessel.

Fresco in the Tomb of the Infernal Chariot, in the Necropolis of Pianacce, Sarteano.

In interpreting images and objects from burials, we have to think of the context of their use. Who entered the tomb, and at what time? When a person dies, a vast gulf is left behind. When that person is young and healthy, there is an element of shock; when they are elderly, a lifetime of memories, remembered with sadness or a smile. When that death is violent, there is an element of fear. Each death leaves behind a specific void. Tradition and belief, however, offer a modicum of control. The format of a funeral provides a chance for relatives to take back some agency from death, to order things as they choose. In providing for the dead we can see a balancing act in which the living simultaneously deal with immediate loss and face the certainty of their own mortality. Etruscan tombs were used by families over an extended period of time for multiple internments, so they were regular venues for this elaborate negotiation of emotions. At Sarteano, we have a remarkably well-preserved

Detail from the Tomb of the Infernal Chariot, Sarteano.

insight into what one family felt they needed to provide for their dead relatives, and what they wanted or needed to encounter in these inevitable moments of intense stress.

First, the necropolis itself. The Pianacce necropolis had been used as a place for the dead for a long period of time, containing tombs that dated from the sixth to the second centuries BCE. In other Etruscan cities, too, burial places have a distinct longevity of use. It was important to these people to return to the same locations to bury the generations of dead, and these locations are outside of towns, often on opposing spurs. At Sarteano, the tombs face southwest and lie on the edge of a hillside, just before a steep drop downwards through modern olive groves. Since the discovery of the tomb in 2003, excavations have continued at the site, revealing a further phase of the burial ritual as practised here. During the 2007 excavation season a strange semi-circular structure steadily emerged from the soil.[6] Built at the centre of the Pianacce necropolis was a deliberately public space, created from great travertine hunks, which was used for the ritual of prothesis – the laying out of the dead. Thought to date from the fifth century BCE, it is akin to a theatre, displaying the dead to the assembled mourners, and, like a theatre, this is the stage for a cathartic release.[7]

The precious painted tomb, known as the Tomb of the Infernal Chariot, dates from the fourth century BCE, after the construction of this formal space. So we can speculate that the deceased were transported from their homes to this central space, probably in a formal procession.[8] Once the laying out was completed, the bodies were interred, placed into the ground. This particular family tomb was constructed after the religious shift described in the previous chapter, but not long after. As a result, the paintings and grave goods of the tomb speak eloquently of a time of conflicting beliefs, a time of change. There is a tension between the implied merriment of the wine service and the vipers on the wall. Some paintings hold true to older ideas of what it means to be dead, and to thoughts of what the afterlife might be like: there remains the two men reclining together, as though at a luxurious banquet. This is a motif we know well from across the Etruscan world, and it continued to be a key idea in defining the afterlife experience. The sarcophagus itself repeats this idea, part of a tradition of burial urns that show the deceased ready to dine out for eternity.[9]

The problem here is that the painted diners are no longer relaxed and happy. Their expressions are forlorn, worried. The two represent an older and a younger man: perhaps father and son, although it has been suggested that they are lovers.[10] They seem uncomfortable and on edge, surrounded by dangers. Rich enough to commission and outfit this tomb, its owners were undeniably anxious about the prospect of the underworld. It is possible that the images of demons served as a protective measure for the deceased. After hundreds of years of valuables being placed in tombs, the owners of this sepulchre were aware of the potential for grave robbery. Perhaps by placing terrifying visions that would loom out of the darkness they hoped to deter any would-be thieves. Possibly these individual beings are intended to be less frightening than

Two gladiators fighting: the Etruscan-inspired figure of Dis Pater/Charun may have been waiting in the wings to finish off the loser.

they appear to us: rather, their strangeness is an additional layer of security, a protection against human thieves and inhuman malevolence. The dead are vulnerable; the living, entering into their realm temporarily, even more so. Returning safely to the living world, without bringing the miasma of the tomb into the home, the burial party might be assured by the presence of these figures who define the boundaries between who is dead and who is alive.

The identity of these beings is not entirely clear. The red-haired demon could be a local incarnation of Charun, the kind of being who controls entry into the afterlife, or could be a female equivalent. Other images of Charun show him as a nightmare figure, carrying a vast hammer. He appears in ceramic art behind prisoners about to be executed, or warriors fallen in battle. Disturbingly, Charun has counterparts, ready to strike anywhere at any time – there are at least four gathered together in a tomb from Cerveteri. These demons can be shown with menacing hybrid features from the animal world: the countenance of a wolf, or sharp tusks of a boar.[11] He can also be shown with ailments that would cause death to a human being: one of the four figures from Cerveteri is shown with hideously blistered skin, as though burnt.[12] The figure of Charun made a deep impression on the psyche of his victims, and the image would survive as a dark part of the Romans' Etruscan inheritance: gladiatorial combat. The rechristened figure of 'Dis Pater' would emerge once the battles were over, a masked man carrying a huge hammer used to finish off the wounded and ensure that the dead stayed dead. The continuity is clear: once Charun has got you, there is no going back.

The snakes, too, are attested elsewhere. They seem to be venomous adders, although the mouths full of fangs are more like those of a dragon than any living serpent. More conventional serpents appear wrapped around the arms of a demon from a contemporaneous tomb at Tarquinia: his skin is coloured blue, the same shade that a person bitten by an adder would turn as they fought the snake's poison.[13] The snake's presence here is appropriate as another figure who chooses the dead. Three heads, perhaps to emphasize the importance of the tripartite nature of the ritual journey into the underworld: the living, the freshly dead and the buried. The identity of the red-headed demon remains unclear: perhaps it is a more locally relevant deity. Not represented is the female death demon Vanth, who is paired with Charun at the Francois Tomb in Vulci, overseeing the slaughter of prisoners, and on either side of the doors in the Tomb of the Anina Family in Tarquinia. She is also regularly represented in sculpture, usually as a harbinger of death rather than a feature of the afterlife itself.[14] Perhaps this explains her absence, and that of Charun, from the Tomb of the Infernal Chariot; perhaps it is simply personal or regional preferences in frightening death divinities. In all these examples, however, the pattern is the same: from images of a luxuriant afterlife of myriad pleasures, Etruscan mourners chose to encounter increasingly frightening scenes as they buried their loved ones.

It is tempting to connect this new negativity in Etruscan tomb paintings to political events. The wars between Roman armies and various Etruscan cities were long and drawn out, with a dark pattern of sieges and slaughter emerging. The archaeology, however, suggests that Etruscan communities survived this period: surveys reveal the continuity of rural settlements, while the survival of late objects like the Piacenza Liver illustrates the strength of Etruscan cultural beliefs in the new Roman world.[15] Bilingual inscriptions, personal haruspices, Etruscan imperial brides, the wild popularity of gladiatorial games, even the toga: Etruscan culture seeped steadily into Rome.[16] However, as foreshadowed in the horror-struck tones of Tertullian,[17] vocalizing the threat Etruscan religion posed to Christianity, the death demons of Sarteano and their fellows would remain in the subconscious of future generations of Tuscans. The negativity of later Etruscan families towards the afterlife would be their bequest to their descendants, adding a sinister shadow to the already established myth of the mysterious Etruscan.

The reappearance of these monstrous Etruscans is visible at the beginning of the Italian Renaissance, in the paintings of the artist Giotto (*c.* 1267–1337). A native Florentine, the master painter's most famous work lies in Padua, where he was commissioned by the extraordinarily wealthy Scrovegni family to decorate their private chapel, completed in 1305. The Scrovegnis had made their money from banking, with the sin of usury filling their coffers. Giotto's paintings were part of an attempt to mend the Scrovegnis' tattered relationship with God.[18] However, arching over the entranceway is a terrifying vision of the Last Judgement, perhaps not the most subtle subject for a patron whose father was included in the contemporary Dante's inhabitants of *Inferno*. In the bottom right-hand corner, Satan squats with arms outstretched, reaching and grabbing his victims and bringing them to his merciless mouth. It is a scene deeply reminiscent of an Etruscan tomb painting from Tarquinia, and this Tuscan devil is complete with blue skin and adders wrapped around his arms. The snakes from Sarteano have a new home in a new Christian hell. These most frightening aspects of late Etruscan death-belief died hard.

It was not only Renaissance artists who thought to revitalize the Etruscan dead to terrify the living. Italian horror cinema resurrected them too. *The Vampires*, released in 1957, features a female villainess, a theme that would be returned to in the 1960s in *Black*

Sunday and *The Mask of the Demon*, and continued to pop up through the decade in *The Long Hair of Death* (1964) and *Kill Baby Kill* (1966, titled *Operazione Paura*, 'Operation Fear', in Italian). Seductively beautiful yet entirely evil, these terrifying women evoke the horror in Greek texts that speak of Etruscan women and their power, and the disgust of Roman authors describing interfering mothers and the poisoning wives of emperors. They are an oblique echo of these ancient fears, but more obvious references to the Etruscan past appeared as Italian horror began to branch out in the early 1970s. *L'Etrusco uccide ancora*, marketed in English as *The Dead are Alive*, was released in 1973. It features a pair of archaeologists who tangle with a vengeful Etruscan demon. It seems that the furious spirit is responsible for a series of grisly murders – naturally assisted by an army of Etruscan zombies. Another nosy archaeologist is punished in the cringe-worthy *Burial Ground: The Nights of Terror* (*Notti del terrore*), produced in 1981. As he excavates alone by night (of course) the Etruscan dead rise from the earth, with fatal consequences. Almost exactly the same plotline was repeated once again in *Assassinio al cimitero Etrusco* (The Scorpion with Two Tails), released in 1982, with added possession by Etruscan goddesses and a neat twist involving a drug deal gone wrong.

While these films are largely unknown outside Italy, they mark a continued role for the Etruscans as frightening menaces from beyond the grave. The late Etruscan representation of demons, when combined with Christian portraits of vicious priests demanding the martyrdom of the faithful, made for a potent gothic cocktail. This perception of dead Etruscans as eternally seeking out revenge for their supposed 'lost civilization' has also trickled into European and American horror, and remains current in even the latest supernatural teen thrillers. In the classic 1976 film *The Omen*, the parents of the devil-child Damien discover his mother's burial place – in an Etruscan necropolis, naturally. The 2006 remake introduced the dangerous dead Etruscan woman to a new generation, but it was the *Twilight* franchise that would bring Etruscan death magic to the attention of thousands of teenage fans. The revelation that the Etruscan city of Volterra was the ancient home of the government of a secret network of vampires emphasized the continued power of the legendary figure of the mysterious Etruscan and brought a rush of visitors to this beautiful hill city, all in search of the reinvented Etruscan past and a Tuscan vampire of their very own.

Etruscan demons clung on through centuries of Christianity to resurface in Padua, and in Italian cinema, but many remains of those who originally believed in their power did not. Etruria was, and remains, one of the richest hunting grounds for tomb robbers, and gangs of looters emptied the vast majority of Etruscan burials. This is still a problem today, although as museums have become fussier about provenances, looters' finds have ended up on auction websites and the dark side of the Internet, to be flogged to private collectors. The *tombaroli* themselves have become a subject for study: one gave an interview to an interested archaeologist explaining the deep familiarity he felt with those whose tombs he repeatedly invaded.[19] He felt that the Etruscan gods were indeed watching him, as they do in Italian horror cinema, except that they were benevolent. He described how on some nights he could feel the Etruscans calling to him. The dead bodies themselves, their dry bones and crumbled burnt pieces, were dumped out of sarcophagi and scattered on the floor; strangely enough, in calling to the *tombarolo* the dead Etruscans did not protest this treatment. It is only in recent years that intact burials are being found in numbers great enough for archaeologists to begin answering personal questions about the people whose possessions they have been lining up and analysing for so long.

One of the most recent, and most detailed, studies comes from an Etruscan new town, Spina, just to the south of the Venetian lagoon. A team of scholars from the nearby University of Ferrara looked at 303 skeletons.[20] The burials ranged in date from the sixth to the third centuries, and included the bodies of men, women and children. The results were surprising: these people had a good standard of health, and a relatively late average age of death, if they were fortunate enough to survive childhood. This is almost a decade older than later Roman populations: the inhabitants of Spina were lucky. There were signs that the women buried here suffered from anaemia brought on by a lack of iron sufficient to compensate for the demands of menstruation, pregnancy and breastfeeding. Both men and women would have known the aches and pains of arthritis, but the male bodies were more severely afflicted, particularly in the hip and the elbow joints. That they lived long enough to develop the tell-tale signs of these problems is a testament to their good health: the younger individuals died of more serious illnesses which left no trace on their bones, sweeping away previously healthy individuals in a lightning strike.

The familiarization of the Etruscan dead does not take place solely through this kind of medically orientated study. Their faces, too, can emerge when the physical remains are placed in the spotlight of archaeological analysis. The skeleton of a woman, preserved in her beautifully decorated sarcophagus in the British Museum, not only gave up the story of her life, but allowed the reconstruction of her face. Seianti Hanunia Tlesnasa was buried in the second century BCE, and her serene gaze is as compelling as on the day her likeness was placed in the ground.[21] Her coffin was topped with a portrait sculpture, showing a mature woman reclining on a dining bench, supported by soft pillows. The face itself is full and fleshy, with sensuous lips and the hint of a double chin. The nose is distinctly pudgy. Was this a standardized figure, or was this the face of the woman buried in the sarcophagus it crowned? As her features emerged from the layers of clay used to reconstruct her facial muscles, it became clear that this was a portrait. The real Seianti was as full-featured and distinctive as her eternal double. The resemblance was obvious, but so too was the flattery that is inherent in the portrait as art. Seianti's sarcophagus showed a memory of a beautiful woman in the bloom of her life, while her face showed a more weathered countenance. This face is not that of a mysterious Etruscan, some spooky creature back from the dead: it is entirely ordinary and familiar.

It would be wonderful to be able to undertake facial reconstruction on all Etruscan skeletons where the skull survives. However, while seeing the faces of the dead may make for a reminder of their humanity, it is not the only way that the bodies of the Etruscans themselves are transforming the way we think about them. New discoveries are emerging all the time, including of undisturbed tombs where the inhabitants remain. In late 2015, the bones of three or even four adults were found in a new tomb at Casal di Pari, a tiny village in central Tuscany.[22] Analysis is just beginning on these new Etruscans, and reanalysis is starting on the bones that have survived from older excavations. The potential of 3D printing to allow wider dissemination of these remains is one aspect of their potential, while the growing complexity and efficiency of DNA analysis is another. With improvements in the extraction of ancient DNA, it could be possible to track family relationships through different burials, and potentially different sites, as well as through time. Seeing the links of mothers, fathers, daughters and sons brings home the reality that these were once living people, not demons, zombies or questions to be answered.

This book began with one tomb, and ends with another. Sadly, in both cases, the physical remains of the Etruscans who occupied the Tomb of the Infernal Chariot, and the *Sarcophagus of the Spouses*, are long lost. We will never be able to find out if the people buried beneath those enigmatic figures matched up to their ceramic doubles, whether they had children together, whether they died young and beautiful like their portraits, or were instead old and crotchety. But we will know these things about their fellow Etruscans, who shared life and afterlife with them. Our knowledge will grow year on year and decade by decade, slowly and steadily eroding the myth of the mysterious Etruscans. The great questions may be answered by new finds or new ideas: maybe an Etruscan Rosetta stone lies hidden away beneath the Italian earth just waiting to be discovered, maybe a DNA technique will be developed that can untangle the intricacies of the Etruscan genome and settle the origins debate.

It is a deeply exciting time to be alive, and to be interested in those who are dead. This book has followed the stories and the study of one group of communities of pre-Roman Italy, one culture among a world filled with diversity and fascination, past and present. The perceived strangeness of the Etruscans, their place between Greece and Rome, places them in a unique position in the history of the world. At the start of this book, I argued for the existence of a false dichotomy between 'lost civilizations' and people 'just like us'. Both these positions are impossible to maintain.

It is the intoxicating mixture of familiarity and strangeness, the bizarre and the cosy, that makes the study of this complex, fascinating, frustrating people so worthwhile. In spite of the destroyed tombs, the damaged texts and the mangled genes, all it takes is one look into the eyes of the *Sarcophagus of the Spouses* and something magical happens. We gaze into the past and we see the future. The Etruscans make us question who we are, where we come from and where we are going. To study them is to examine the most important questions of the modern world, and attempt to answer them on behalf of a people who speak only through things they left behind. Someday, the very same task may be confronting archaeologists working on twenty-first-century archaeology, left without texts after some mass digital failure, seeking the truth about ancestors whose lives have become legend. This is not a Lost Civilization, hidden in a tangled jungle of myth and rumour, inhabited by a shadowy buried people. The Etruscan world is there to be rediscovered through the vibrant lives of its citizens and the remarkable objects they made, and you can be a part of this great enterprise.

REFERENCES

Prologue

1 T.B.M.B. Macaulay, *Lays of Ancient Rome* (London, 1895).

1 Why do the Etruscans Matter?

1 See B. Bosio and A. Pugnetti, eds, *Gli Etruschi di Cerveteri, catalogo della mostra* (Modena, 1986); A. Coen, *Complessi tombali di Cerveteri con urne cinerarie tardo-orientalizzanti* (Rome, 1991); M. Cristofani, *Cerveteri: tre itinerari archeologici* (Rome, 1991); G. B. Gianni, ed., *Cerveteri: importazioni e contesti nelle necropoli: una lettura sperimentale di alcune tombe nelle Civiche Raccolte Archeologiche e Nusmismatiche di Milano* (Milan, 2002); R. Marconi Cosentino, *Cerveteri e il suo territorio. Guide Territoriali dell'Etruria Meridionale* (Rome, 1995).

2 G. Nadalini, 'Le musée Campana: origine et formation des collections', in *L'anticomanie: La collection d'antiquités aux 18e et 19e siècles. Colloque international, Montpellier-Lattes, 9–12 juin 1988*, ed. A. Laurens (Paris, 1992), pp. 111–23.

3 D. Magri and L. Sadori, 'Late Pleistocene and Holocene Pollen Stratigraphy at Lago di Vico, Central Italy', *Vegetation History and Archaeobotany*, 8 (1999), pp. 247–60. See also L. Sadori et al., 'Reconstructing Past Cultural Landscape and Human Impact Using Pollen and Plant Macroremains', *Plant Biosystems*, 144 (2010), pp. 940–51; C. Bellini et al., 'Plant Gathering and Cultivation in Prehistoric Tuscany (Italy)', *Vegetation History and Archaeobotany*, 17 (2008), pp. 103–12.

4 M. Mariotti Lippi et al., 'Archaeobotanical Investigations into an Etruscan Farmhouse at Pian d'Alma (Grosseto, Italy)', *Atti della Societa Toscana di Scienza Naturale*, 109 (2003), pp. 159–65.

5 See G. Barker, 'Archaeology and the Etruscan Countryside', *Antiquity*, 62 (1988), pp. 772–8, and G. Barker, 'The Archaeology of the Italian Shepherd', *Proceedings of the Cambridge Philological Society (New Series)*, 35 (1989), pp. 1–19; T. W. Potter, *The Changing Landscape of South Etruria* (London, 1979); J. B. Ward-Perkins, 'Etruscan Towns, Roman Roads

and Medieval Villages: The Historical Geography of Southern Etruria', *Geographical Journal*, 128 (1962), pp. 389–404; P. Perkins and I. Attolini, 'An Etruscan Farm at Podere Tartuchino', *Papers of the British School at Rome*, 60 (1992), pp. 71–134, chronicles the excavation of a rare Etruscan farmstead at Podere Tartuchino.

6 For the sedimentation of the Tiber delta, see J. P. Goiran et al., 'Geoarchaeology Confirms Location of the Ancient Harbour Basin of Ostia (Italy)', *Journal of Archaeological Science*, 41 (2014), pp. 389–98.

2 Where is Home?

1 See J. Robb, *The Early Mediterranean Village: Agency, Material Culture, and Social Change in Neolithic Italy* (Cambridge, 2007), p. 60, and J. Robb, 'Burial and Social Reproduction in the Peninsular Italian Neolithic', *Journal of Mediterranean Archaeology*, 7 (1994), pp. 27–71, for burial practices in the Italian Neolithic.

2 A. Barra et al., 'La Grotta Continenza di Trasacco. I livelli e le ceramiche', *Rivista di scienze preistoriche*, 42 (1989), pp. 31–100.

3 V. Pesce Delfino et al., 'Tomba megalitica in camera del III millenio in Rutigliano (Bari): triplice deposizione', *Antropologia Contemporanea*, 2 (1979), pp. 453–7.

4 G. A. Piga et al., 'Anthropological and Physicochemical Investigation of the Burnt Remains of Tomb IX in the "Sa Figu" Hypogeal Necropolis (Sassari, Italy) – Early Bronze Age', *International Journal of Osteoarchaeology*, 18 (2008), pp. 167–77.

5 G. Bartolini, *Le urne a capanna rinvenute in Italia* (Rome, 1987); R. Leighton, 'House Urns and Etruscan Tomb Painting: Tradition Versus Innovation in the Ninth–Seventh Centuries BC', *Oxford Journal of Archaeology*, 24 (2005), pp. 363–80.

6 A. Boethius, R. Ling and T. Rasmussen, eds, *Etruscan and Early Roman Architecture* (New Haven, CT, 1978).

7 H. G. Harke, *Settlement Types and Settlement Patterns in the West Hallstatt Province: An Evaluation of Evidence from Excavated Sites* (Oxford, 1979); N. Roymans, 'The Cultural Biography of Urnfields and the Long-term History of a Mythical Landscape', *Archaeological Dialogues*, 2 (1995), pp. 2–24; H. Fokkens, 'The Genesis of Urnfields: Economic Crisis or Ideological Change?', *Antiquity*, 71 (1997), pp. 360–73.

8 A. Fioravanti et al., *L'abitato villanoviano del Gran Carro sommerso nel lago di Bolsena (1959–1977)* (Rome, 1977).

9 A. Comella, *Il deposito votivo presso l'Ara della Regina. Materiali del Museo Archeologico Nazionale di Tarquinia* (Rome, 1982). See the collected works of Maria Bonghi Jovino for more on Tarquinia: M. Bonghi Jovino, 'Gli scavi nell'abitato di Tarquinia e la scoperta dei "bronzi" in un preliminare inquadramento', in *Tarquinia-ricerche, scavi e prospettive: Atti del convegno internazionale di studi La Lombardia per gli Etruschi*, ed. M. Bonghi Jovino and C. Chiaramonte Trerè (Milan, 1986),

pp. 59–77; M. Bonghi Jovino, *Tarquinia: scavi sistematici nell'abitato, campagne 1982–1988: i materiali* (Rome, 2001); M. Bonghi Jovino, 'The Tarquinia Project: A Summary of 25 Years of Excavation', *American Journal of Archaeology*, 114 (2010), pp. 161–80.

10 Herodotus, *Histories*, 1.96; see R. Drews, 'Herodotus 1.94, the Drought ca. 1200 BC, and the Origin of the Etruscans', *Historia: Zeitschrift fur Alte Geschichte*, 41 (1992), pp. 14–39; R.S.P. Beekes, *The Origin of the Etruscans* (Amsterdam, 2008).

11 Livy, *History of Rome*, book 5.

12 Pliny the Elder, *Natural History*, book 7:2; see C. Gabli, 'Pliny the Elder on the Etruscans', *Acta Ant Hung*, 52 (2012), pp. 137–63.

13 Tacitus, *Annals*, book 7.

14 Ibid., book 1:30.

15 Tacitus, *Histories*, book 5.

16 H. C. Winther, 'Princely Tombs of the Orientalizing Period in Etruria and Latium Vetus', in *Urbanization in the Mediterranean in the 9th to 6th Centuries BC*, ed. H. Damgaard Andersen (Copenhagen, 1997), pp. 423–46.

17 J. P. Oleson, 'Technical Aspects of Etruscan Rock-cut Tomb Architecture', *Römische Mitteilungen*, 85 (1978), pp. 283–314; V. Izzet, 'Engraving the Boundaries: Exploring Space and Surface in Etruscan Funerary Architecture', in *Approaches to the Study of Ritual: Italy and the Ancient Mediterranean*, ed. J. Wilkins (London, 1996), pp. 55–72.

18 D. Ridgway, 'George Dennis and the Etruscans', *Antiquity*, 48 (1974), pp. 190–95; D. E. Rhodes, *Dennis of Etruria: The Life of George Dennis* (London, 1973).

19 C. Denina, *Delle rivoluzioni d'Italia libri ventiquattro* (Rome, 1769).

20 G. Q. Giglioli, *L'arte etrusca* (Milan, 1935).

21 M. Pallottino, 'Sulle facies culturali arcaiche dell'Etruria', *Studi Etruschi*, 13 (1939), p. 86.

22 P. Francalacci et al., 'Sequence Diversity of the Control Region of Mitochondrial DNA in Tuscany and its Implications for the Peopling of Europe', *American Journal of Physical Anthropology*, C/4 (1996), pp. 443–60.

23 B. A. Malyarchuk and I. B. Rogozin, 'On the Etruscan Mitochondrial DNA Contribution to Modern Humans', *American Journal of Human Genetics*, LXXV/5 (2004), pp. 920–23.

24 M. Pellecchia et al., 'The Mystery of Etruscan Origins: Novel Clues from Bos Taurus Mitochondrial DNA', *Proceedings of the Royal Society of London B: Biological Sciences*, 274 (2007), pp. 1175–9.

25 A. Achilli et al., 'Mitochondrial DNA Variation of Modern Tuscans Supports the Near Eastern Origin of Etruscans', *American Journal of Human Genetics*, LXXX (2007), pp. 759–68.

26 Philip Perkins discusses the issues with these genetic studies in detail: P. Perkins, 'DNA and Etruscan Identity', in *Etruscan by Definition: Papers in Honour of Sybille Haynes*, ed. P. Perkins and J. Swaddling (London, 2009), pp. 95–112.

27 This data is open access. Please do read S. Ghirotto et al., 'Origins and Evolution of the Etruscans' mtDNA', *PloS One*, VIII/2 (2013).

3 Ostrich Eggs and Oriental Dreams

1 See A. M. Moretti Sgubini, *Vulci e il suo territorio* (Rome, 1993); 'Scoperte e iniziative in Etruria Meridionale', *Etruscan Studies*, 9 (2002), pp. 133–52; 'Alle origini di Vulci', in *Archeologia in Etruria meridionale*, ed. M. Pandolfini Angeletti (Rome, 2006), pp. 317–61. The classic description of late nineteenth-century excavations at Vulci is S. Gsell, *Fouilles dans la nécropole de Vulci* (Paris, 1891).

2 Their website, www.britishmuseum.ac.uk, provides an excellent introduction to the tomb, its contents and history.

3 S. Haynes, 'The Isis Tomb: Do its Contents Form a Consistent Group?', in *La civilta arcaica di Vulci e la sua espressione: Atti del X convengo di Studi Etruschi ed Italichi*, ed. A. Neppi Modona (Florence, 1977), pp. 17–30 considers the collection of these objects, and assesses the likelihood of their shared provenance of this single tomb.

4 C. Riva, *The Urbanisation of Etruria: Funerary Practices and Social Change, 700–600 BC* (Cambridge, 2010) provides the most up-to-date synthesis of this important period, but see also A. Naso, 'The Etruscan Aristocracy in the Orientalizing Period: Culture, Economy, Relations', in *The Etruscans*, ed. M. Torelli (London, 2001), pp. 111–29. For the wider Mediterranean context, see A. C. Gunter, 'Orientalism and Orientalization in the Iron Age Mediterranean', in *Critical Approaches to Ancient Near Eastern Art*, ed. B. Brown and M. Feldman (New York, 2013), pp. 78–108; and for Greece see A. C. Gunter, *Greek Art and the Orient* (Cambridge, 2009), and W. Burkert and M. E. Pinder, *The Orientalizing Revolution: Near Eastern Influence on Greek Culture in the Early Archaic Age* (Boston, MA, 1995).

5 See also T. Rasmussen, 'Urbanization in Etruria', in *Mediterranean Urbanization, 800–600 BC*, ed. R. Osborne and B. Cunliffe (Oxford, 2005), pp. 71–90, and H. Damgaard Andersen, 'The Archaeological Evidence for the Development of the Etruscan City in the 7th to 6th centuries BC', in *Urbanization in the Mediterranean in the 9th to 6th Centuries BC*, ed. H. Damgaard Andersen (Copenhagen, 1997), pp. 343–82.

6 S. W. Silliman, 'Culture Contact or Colonialism? Challenges in the Archaeology of Native North America', *American Antiquity*, LXX (2005), pp. 55–74, examines the archaeology of contact and exploitation in a North American context, while L. Tuhiwai Smith, *Decolonizing Methodologies: Research and Indigenous Peoples* (London, 1999) considers the deep heritage of such exploitative behaviour on research practice.

7 Lin Foxhall explains this as 'the desire for things, especially foreign things, which convey meanings to and on the consumer and his or her social circle', in L. Foxhall, 'Village to City: Staples and Luxuries?

Exchange Networks and Urbanization', in *Mediterranean Urbanization, 800–600 BC*, pp. 233–48.

8 R. Tykot, 'Sea Peoples in Etruria? Italian Contacts with the Eastern Mediterranean in the Late Bronze Age', *Etruscan Studies*, I (1994), pp. 59–83, summarizes these.

9 E. Said, *Orientalism* (London, 1978), and 'Representing the Colonized: Anthropology's Interlocutors', *Critical Inquiry*, XV (1989), pp. 205–25.

10 A. Schom, *Napoleon Bonaparte: A Life* (London, 1998) provides an excellent biography of Napoleon, while his extraordinary rise to power is chronicled by R. Asprey in *The Rise of Napoleon Bonaparte* (London, 2000). They both consider Lucien's relationship with his brother.

11 Lucien Bonaparte himself chronicled his Etruscan finds in his *Catalogo di scelte antichità Etrusche trovate negli scavi del principe di Canino, 1828–1829* (Rome, 1829), while the exhibition catalogue of a recent display of his surviving finds contextualizes their discovery. See G. M. Della Fina, ed., *Citazioni archeologiche: Luciano Bonaparte archeologo, catalogo della Mostra, Orvieto, Museo Claudio Faina, 10 settembre 2004–9 gennaio 2005* (Rome, 2004).

12 See P. Strathern, *Napoleon in Egypt: 'The Greatest Glory'* (London, 2008) for Napoleon's Egyptian campaigns, and D. M. Reid, *Whose Pharaohs? Archaeology, Museums, and Egyptian National Identity from Napoleon to World War I* (Berkeley, CA, 2002) for an assessment of their role in shaping Egyptology.

13 For the Napoleonic context and archaeology, see S. Woolf, 'The Construction of a European World-view in the Revolutionary-Napoleonic Years', *Past and Present*, CXXXVII (1992), pp. 72–101; M. Diaz-Andreu, 'Guest Editor's Introduction: Nationalism and Archaeology', *Nations and Nationalism*, VII (2001), pp. 429–40, expands on the theme of nineteenth-century nationalism, the Enlightenment and archaeology.

14 This view is vocalized by Dennis: 'No fact can be more clearly established than the oriental character of the civic and religious polity, the social and domestic manners, and many of the arts of the Etruscans; and traces of this affinity are abundant in their monuments.' G. Dennis, *The Cities and Cemeteries of Etruria* (London, 1889), p. 38.

15 The word 'princely' is still used, albeit in quotation marks, in modern analyses of these burials: see, for example, G. Bartoloni, ed., *Principi etruschi tra Mediterraneo ed Europa* (Milan, 2000), and V. Belleli, 'La tomba "principesca" dei Quattordici Ponti nel contesto di Capua arcaica', *Studia Archaeologica*, CXLII (2006), p. 174.

16 C. Smith, *The Roman Clan: The Gens from Ancient Ideology to Modern Anthropology* (Cambridge, 2006) is focused on the role of elites and families in state formation in the relevant context of early Rome.

17 Namely that of K. Kreindler, *Consumption and Exchange in Central Italy in the Ninth through Sixth Centuries BCE* (Stanford, CA, 2015).

4 Pots and Prejudice

1 D. Paleothodoros, 'Archaeological Contexts and Iconographic Analysis: Case Studies from Greece and Etruria', in *The World of Greek Vases*, ed. V. Nørskov, L. Hannestad, C. Isler-Kerényi and S. Lewis (Rome, 2008), pp. 45–62, esp. p. 50, examines a wide range of Greek ceramics and supports this conclusion.

2 For the history of excavations at Chiusi, see M. Iozzo, *Materiali dimenticati, memorie recuperate: restauri e acquisizioni nel Museo Archeologico Nazionale di Chiusi* (Chiusi, 2007); G. Paolucci, *Documenti e memorie sulle antichità e il Museo di Chiusi* (Pisa, 2005).

3 R. d'Arezzo, *La composizione del mondo di Ristoro d'Arezzo: testo italiano del 1282* (Rome, 1872), p. 137.

4 G. Bartoloni and P. Bocci Pacini, 'The Importance of Etruscan Antiquity in the Tuscan Renaissance', *Acta Hyperborea: Danish Studies in Classical Archaeology*, 10 (2003), pp. 449–72; G. Cipriani, *Il mito etrusco nel rinascimento fiorentino* (Florence, 1980), p. 17.

5 A. M. Galdy, *Cosimo I de' Medici as Collector: Antiquities and Archaeology in Sixteenth-century Florence* (Cambridge, 2009), p. 42.

6 The significance of the Guarnacci museum is expressed by C. Duggan in *The Force of Destiny: A History of Italy Since 1796* (London, 2008), p. 29.

7 J. J. Winckelmann, *Histoire de l'art chez anciens* (Paris, 1802).

8 J. J. Winckelmann and A. Potts, *The History of the Art of Antiquity* (Los Angeles, CA, 2006).

9 V. Izzet, 'Greeks Make It; Etruscans Fecit: The Stigma of Plagiarism in the Reception of Etruscan Art', *Etruscan Studies*, x (2007), pp. 223–37, considers Winckelmann's relationship with Etruscan art at length.

10 J. J. Winckelmann, quoted by V. Izzet, ibid., p. 227.

11 Ibid., p. 222.

12 P. H. d'Hancarville, *Collection of Etruscan, Greek, and Roman Antiquities from the Cabinet of the Hon. W. Hamilton his Britannick Maiesty's Envoy Extraordinary at the Court of Naples* (London, 1766).

13 The bibliography of Greek vase studies is vast and fascinating. A good starting point is B. Sparkes, *The Red and the Black: Studies in Greek Pottery* (London, 2013). Of course, the giant of twentieth-century vase studies was the great Sir John Beazley, for a flavour of whose great work see J. D. Beazley, *Attic Red-figure Vase-painters* (Oxford, 1963) or J. D. Beazley, *Attic Black-figure Vase-painters* (Oxford, 1978).

14 *Hymn to Dionysus*, 6–8. The Etruscans are also represented as pirates by Thucydides, *History of the Peloponnesian War* (1.5.1).

15 Herodotus, *Histories*, 1.166–7.

16 The vehement disapproval of all things Etruscan is voiced most strongly by J. Boardman in *The Greeks Overseas* (Oxford, 1964), pp. 210–11.

17 This view has its origins within the classical sources. Diodorus Siculus (*Biblioteca historica*, 5.40.3) waxes lyrical over the fertility of Etruria,

while Livy's *History of Rome* is peppered with instances of Etruscan cities providing grain to hungry Rome (9.41.5 and 28.45.15). P. Bernardini and G. Camporeale, *The Etruscans Outside Etruria* (Los Angeles, CA, 2004), p. 33, states that 'the abundance of primary resources in the region was the driving force behind the intense trade activity of the Etruscans, both on land and on the sea.'

18 This view is developed from the linguistic evidence, for which see F. Adratos, 'More on Etruscan as an IE-Anatolian Language', *Historische Sprachforschung/Historical Linguistics*, 107 (1994), pp. 54–76, and C. de Simone, 'La Nuova Iscrizione "Tirsenica" di Lemnos (Efestia, teatro): considerazioni generali', *Rasenna: Journal of the Center for Etruscan Studies*, III (2011), pp. 1–34.

19 For the Marseilles region, see M. Bats, 'Marseille archaïque. Étrusques et Phocéens en Méditerranée nord-occidentale', *Mélanges de l'Ecole française de Rome, Antiquité*, 110 (1998), pp. 609–33; M. Dietler, *Archaeologies of Colonialism: Consumption, Entanglement, and Violence in Ancient Mediterranean France* (Berkeley, CA, 2010), explores Etruscan influence in the wider region of southern France.

20 K. Lomas, 'Beyond Magna Graecia: Greeks and Non-Greeks in France, Spain and Italy', in *The Blackwell Companion to the Ancient World*, ed. K. Kinzi (London, 2006), pp. 174–96, esp. p. 184, outlines the activity of Greek and Etruscan traders within Spain.

21 For *kantharoi*, see H.A.G. Brijder, 'The Shapes of Etruscan Bronze Kantharoi from the Seventh Century BC and the Earliest Attic Black-figure Kantharoi', *BaBesch*, LXIII (1988), pp. 103–14. For Etruscan shapes in Greece more widely see T. Rasmussen, 'Etruscan shapes in Attic Pottery', *Antike Kunst*, XXVIII (1985), pp. 33–9.

22 Nikosthenes is the subject of numerous works, having been identified by his signature at an early stage. See J. D. Beazley, *Greek Vases: Lectures by J. D. Beazley* (Oxford, 1989), p. 9.

23 The shape seems to originate in Crete: see M. Popham, 'The Late Minoan Goblet and Kylix', *Annual of the British School at Athens*, 64 (1969), pp. 299–304.

24 V. Izzet, 'Greeks Make It; Etruscans Fecit', p. 217.

25 The classic works on bucchero are: T. Rasmussen, *Bucchero Pottery from Southern Etruria* (Cambridge, 2006), and A. Camerini, *Il bucchero etrusco* (Rome, 1985).

26 C. Roth-Murray, *A Disclosure of Power: Elite Etruscan Iconography During the 8th–6th Centuries BC* (Oxford, 2005).

5 Super Rich, Invisible Poor

1 F. Fulminante, *The Urbanisation of Rome and Latium Vetus: From the Bronze Age to the Archaic Era* (Cambridge, 2014) gives the best up-to-date summary of these studies in her work on Latium Vetus, which incorporates the Etruscan data for comparison.

2 These figures are taken from S. Steingraber, 'The Process of Urbanization of Etruscan Settlements from the Late Villanovan to the Late Archaic Period', *Etruscan Studies*, VIII (2001), pp. 7–34, figures on p. 14.
3 See for example P. Perkins and I. Attolini, 'Podere Tartuchino' (1992); V. Izzet, *The Archaeology of Etruscan Society* (Cambridge, 1997), has critiqued the dominance of the funerary record in Etruria, but this imbalance in evidence seems set to continue to bias Etruscan archaeology long into the future.
4 A. S. Tuck, *The Necropolis of Poggio Civitate (Murlo): Burials from Poggio Aguzzo* (Rome, 2011).
5 For Bianchi Bandinelli see M. Barbanera, *Ranuccio Bianchi Bandinelli e il suo mondo* (Bari, 2000), and *Ranuccio Bianchi Bandinelli: biografia ed epistolario di un grande archeologo* (Milan, 2003). This apocryphal story is local and excavation legend.
6 These signs of the Iron Age at Poggio Civitate were presented in poster form by A. S. Tuck et al., *The Iron Age at Poggio Civitate: Evidence and Argument* (American Institute of Archaeology Annual Meeting, 2012).
7 N. Winter, 'Commerce in Exile: Terracotta Roofing in Etruria, Corfu and Sicily, a Bacchiad Family Enterprise', *Etruscan Studies*, IX (2002), pp. 227–38; N. Winter, *Symbols of Wealth and Power: Architectural Terracotta Decoration in Etruria and Central Italy, 640–510 BC* (Rome, 2010). See also P. S. Lulof, 'Archaic Terracotta Acroteria Representing Athena and Heracles: Manifestations of Power in Central Italy', *Journal of Roman Archaeology*, XIII (2000), pp. 207–19.
8 For the Orientalizing period complex, see A. S. Tuck and E. Nielsen, 'An Orientalizing Period Complex at Poggio Civitate (Murlo): A Preliminary View', *Etruscan Studies*, VIII (2001), pp. 35–64.
9 New ivory plaques are still coming to light, some with important inscriptions. See A. S. Tuck and R. Wallace, 'A "New" Inscribed Plaque from Poggio Civitate (Murlo)', *Etruscan Studies*, XV (2012), pp. 1–17; for the bucchero, see J. Berkin, *The Orientalizing Bucchero from the Lower Building at Poggio Civitate (Murlo)* (Philadelphia, PA, 2004); E. Nielsen, 'Bronze Production at Poggio Civitate (Murlo)', *Etruscan Studies*, V (1998), pp. 95–108, considers the production of bronze at Poggio Civitate.
10 Described in A. S. Tuck and R. Wallace, 'Letters and Non-alphabetic Characters on Roof Tiles from Poggio Civitate (Murlo)', *Etruscan Studies*, XVI (2013), pp. 210–62.
11 This narrative of the destruction is drawn from A. S. Tuck and E. Nielsen, 'The Chronological Implications of Reliefware Bucchero at Poggio Civitate', *Etruscan Studies*, XI (2008), pp. 49–66.
12 The gradual exposure of this huge building is described by K. M. Phillips in *In the Hills of Tuscany: Recent Excavations at the Etruscan Site of Poggio Civitate (Murlo, Siena)* (Philadelphia, PA, 1993).
13 Livy describes the Etruscan League on a number of occasions: *History of Rome*, 1.8.3; 4.23.5; 4.61.2; 5.1.5; 5.33.9–10.

14 K. M. Phillips, 'Italic House Models and Etruscan Architectural Terracottas of the Seventh Century BC from Acquarossa and Poggio Civitate, Murlo', *Analecta Romana Instituti Danici*, XIV (1985), pp. 7–16, esp. p. 14; I. Edlund-Berry, 'Ritual Destruction of Cities and Sanctuaries: The "Un-founding" of the Archaic Monumental Building at Poggio Civitate (Murlo)', in *Murlo and the Etruscans: Art and Society in Ancient Etruria*, ed. R. De Puma and J. P. Small (Madison, WI, 1994), pp. 16–28; J. M. Turfa and A. G. Steinmayer, 'Interpreting Early Etruscan Structures: The Question of Murlo', *Papers of the British School at Rome*, 70 (2002), pp. 1–28.

15 A. S. Tuck, 'Manufacturing at Poggio Civitate: Elite Consumption and Social Organization in the Etruscan Seventh Century', *Etruscan Studies*, XVII (2014), pp. 121–39, develops the evidence for elite control of production at the site.

16 For the osteoarchaeology, see S. W. Kansa and Mackinnon, 'Etruscan Economics: Forty-five Years of Faunal Remains from Poggio Civitate', *Etruscan Studies*, XVII (2014), pp. 63–87.

17 This is the point made by E. O'Donoghue in 'The Mute Statues Speak: The Archaic Period Acroteria from Poggio Civitate (Murlo)', *European Journal of Archaeology*, XVI (2013), pp. 268–88.

18 For the throne, see the papers collected in P. von Eles, ed., *Guerriero e sacerdote: autorità e comunità nell'età del ferro a Verucchio: la tomba del Trono* (Florence, 2002).

19 For more on this frieze plaque see M. C. Root, 'An Etruscan Horse Race from Poggio Civitate', *American Journal of Archaeology*, LXXVII (1973), pp. 121–37.

20 P. J. Holliday, 'Processional Imagery in Late Etruscan Funerary Art', *American Journal of Archaeology*, XCIV (1990), pp. 73–90, considers procession imagery across Etruria more widely.

21 A. S. Tuck, 'The Social and Political Context of the 7th Century Architectural Terracottas from Poggio Civitate (Murlo)', in *Deliciae Fictiles III: Architectural Terracottas in Ancient Italy: New Discoveries and Interpretations: Proceedings of the International Conference held at the American Academy in Rome, November 7–8*, ed. I. Edlund-Berry and G. Greco (Oxford, 2002), pp. 130–35, presents this idea.

22 A. S. Tuck et al. describe the discoveries in Vescovado di Murlo in 'Centre and Periphery in Inland Etruria: Poggio Civitate and the Etruscan Settlement in Vescovado di Murlo', *Etruscan Studies*, XII (2007), pp. 215–40.

23 This phase of excavations is presented by Tuck, 'Manufacturing at Poggio Civitate'.

24 A. S. Tuck and L. Shipley, 'Poggio Civitate: Exploring Etruscan Enigmas on the Plain of Treasures', *Current World Archaeology*, 67 (2014), pp. 26–31, examines the issues surrounding these discoveries.

25 The author was lucky enough to be present in the immediate aftermath of the first of these discoveries.

26 This rate comes from M. Golden, 'Did the Ancients Care When Their Children Died?', *Greece and Rome*, XXXV (1988), pp. 152–63, esp. p. 155.
27 M. Liston and S. Rostroff, 'Babies in the Well: Archaeological Evidence for Newborn Disposal in Hellenistic Greece', in *The Oxford Handbook of Childhood and Education in the Classical World*, ed. J. Evans Grubbs and T. Parkin (Oxford, 2013), pp. 62–81.
28 A. S. Tuck, personal correspondence with the author.
29 This is described in detail in A. S. Tuck et al., '2015 Excavations at Poggio Civitate and Vescovado di Murlo', *Etruscan Studies*, XIX (2016), pp. 87–148.

6 To be a Woman

1 For clothing, see L. Bonfante, *Etruscan Dress* (New York, 1975).
2 B. Sandhoff, 'Sexual Ambiguity? Androgynous Imagery in Etruria', *Etruscan Studies*, XIV (2011), pp. 71–96.
3 See M. Conkey and J. Spector, 'Archaeology and the Study of Gender', *Advances in Archaeological Method and Theory*, VII (1984), pp. 1–38.
4 This specific criticism is that of R. Pope and I. Ralston, 'Approaching Sex and Status in Iron Age Britain with Reference to the Nearer Continent', in *Communicating Identity in Italic Iron Age Communities*, ed. H. W. Horsnaes (Oxford, 2011), pp. 26–32.
5 This excellent study is J. Toms, 'The Construction of Gender in Early Iron Age Italy', in *Gender and Italian Archaeology: Challenging the Stereotypes*, ed. R. Whitehouse (Oxford, 1998), pp. 157–79.
6 See M. Gasperetti, 'Tarquinia, scoperta tomba inviolata', *Corriere della Sera* (21 September 2013); M. Gasperetti, 'Tarquinia, il risveglio del principe etrusco', *Corriere della Sera* (22 September 2013); and N. Squires, 'Italian Archaeologists Hail Discovery of Etruscan Warrior Prince's Tomb', *Daily Telegraph* (23 September 2013), for these first accounts of the discovery in Italian and English.
7 A. Pinna, 'E di una donna lo scheletro trova alla Doganaccia', *Viterbo News* (26 September 2013); and T. Ghose, 'Oops! Etruscan Warrior Prince Really a Princess', *Live Science* (18 October 2013), reported on this shift of opinion.
8 This is the term used by A. Mandolesi, 'Tomb 6423: The Tomb of the Hanging Aryballos, Tarquinia', *Etruscan News*, 16 (2014), pp. 1, 6–7; quoted on p. 7. It denies the complexity of women's lives as textile producers as examined by M. Gleba, 'Textile Tools as Indicators of Female Identity in Early Iron Age Italy', in *Communicating Identity in Italic Iron Age Communities*, pp. 26–32.
9 L. Bonfante, 'Etruscan Couples and Their Aristocratic Society', *Women's Studies*, VIII (1981), pp. 157–87.
10 G. Bonfante and L. Bonfante, *The Etruscan Language* (Manchester, 2002), p. 89.
11 E. Keuls, *The Reign of the Phallus: Sexual Politics in Ancient Athens* (Berkeley, CA, 1993) provides perhaps the most evocative description of classical Greek androcentric society.

12 Roman women's lives are richly explored by L. Allason Jones, *Women in Roman Britain* (London, 1989); J. F. Gardner, *Women in Roman Law and Society* (Bloomington, IN, 1991); E. D'Ambra, *Roman Women* (Cambridge, 2007).
13 Livy, *History of Rome*, book 1:57.
14 C. Claassen, 'The Familiar Other: The Pivotal Role of Women in Livy's Narrative of Political Development in Early Rome', *Acta Classica*, XLI (1998), pp. 71–103, explores in more detail the role of women in the construction of Livy's morality.
15 Livy, *History of Rome*, book 1:46–8.
16 Tanaquil is the subject of an extended portrait by G. Meyers, 'Tanaquil: The Conception and Construction of an Etruscan Matron', in *A Companion to the Etruscans*, ed. S. Bell and A. Carpino (New York, 2015), pp. 305–21, who explores these tropes in detail.
17 See J. Hallett, *Fathers and Daughters in Roman Society: Women and the Elite Family* (Princeton, NJ, 2014), pp. 70–74, for a detailed analysis of Tullia's story in the light of Roman views on ideal father–daughter relationships.
18 G. Boccaccio, *De mulieribus claris*, trans. V. Brown (Boston, MA, 2001).
19 N. Goldstone, *Joanna: The Notorious Queen of Naples, Jerusalem and Sicily* (London, 2010) provides a lushly written biography of Joanna of Naples.
20 This viewpoint was first put forward by W. Godshalk, 'Livy's Tullia: A Classical Prototype of Lady Macbeth', *Shakespeare Quarterly*, XVI (1965), pp. 240–41. It has recently been resurrected by J. M. Philo, 'Shakespeare's Macbeth and Livy's Legendary Rome', *Review of English Studies*, X (2015), pp. 89–96, which argues for the connection with Painter.

7 Safe as Houses

1 The title in question is S. von Cles-Reden's *The Buried People: A Study of the Etruscan World* (London, 1955).
2 The over-focus on burial archaeology in Etruria is bemoaned by V. Izzet, *The Archaeology of Etruscan Society* (Cambridge, 2007), p. 90, and noted by H. Damgaard Andersen, 'The Archaeological Evidence for the Development of the Etruscan City in the 7th to 6th centuries BC', in *Urbanization in the Mediterranean in the 9th to 6th centuries BC*, ed. H. Damgaard Andersen (Copenhagen, 1997), pp. 343–82.
3 This name for the city was only recently discovered through analysis of inscriptions from the site. See E. Govi, 'Marzabotto', in *The Etruscan World*, ed. J. M. Turfa (London, 2015), pp. 291–4, analysis on p. 291; E. Govi and G. Sassatelli, *Marzabotto: la casa 1 della regio 4, insula 2* (Bologna, 2010), p. 34. An edited collection of the inscriptions from the site was published by G. Sassatelli and D. Briquel, *Iscrizioni e graffiti della città etrusca di Marzabotto* (Bologna, 1994).
4 For the historical context of Marzabotto's destruction and Celtic expansion, see O. Buchsenschutz et al., 'The Golden Age of the Celtic

Aristocracy in the Fourth and Third Centuries BC', *Annales: Histoire, Sciences Sociales*, 67 (2012), pp. 185–215. See also P. B. Ellis, *Celt and Roman: The Celts of Italy* (London, 1998).

5 E. Govi, ed., *Marzabotto: una città etrusca* (Bologna, 2007); Govi's 'Marzabotto' provides a guide to Marzabotto. D. Vitali et al., *L'acropoli della città etrusca di Marzabotto* (Bologna, 2001), describe excavations on the acropolis area, while G. A. Mansuelli, 'Marzabotto: Dix années de fouilles et recherches', *Mélanges de l'ecole Française de Rome antiquité*, LXXXIV (1972), pp. 111–44, summarizes the excavation of the urban area in the 1960s and early 1970s. G. Baldoni, *La ceramica attica dagli scavi ottocenteschi di Marzabotto* (Bologna, 2009) gives some context of the antiquarian excavations at the site.

6 E. Govi and G. Sassatelli, 'Cults and Foundation Rites in the Etruscan City of Marzabotto', in *Etrusco Ritu: Case Studies in Etruscan Ritual Behaviour*, ed. L. B. van der Meer (Leiden, 2010), pp. 17–27.

7 P. Allison, 'Using the Material and Written Sources: Turn of the Millennium Approaches to Roman Domestic Space', *American Journal of Archaeology*, 105 (2001), pp. 181–206, esp. p. 186, notes the problematic nature of these terminologies: terms such as peristylum were far from universal in their usage by Roman scholars, presumably reflecting vernacular descriptions of homes.

8 L. Donati, *La casa dell'impluvium: architettura etrusca a Roselle* (Rome, 1994).

9 See J. P. Baronio, 'Un architetto per il tempio di Tina a Marzabotto. Studio dell'antico procedimento geometrico-proporzionale utilizzato nel progetto del tempio urbano della città etrusca di Kainua', *Ocnus*, 20 (2012), pp. 9–32, and D. Vitali, 'Le téménos de Tina de la ville étrusque de Marzabotto: entre données de fouilles, hypothèses et certitudes', in *L'âge du fer en Europe: mélanges offerts à Olivier Buchsenschutz*, ed. S. Krausz et al. (Bordeaux, 2013), pp. 583–94, for more on the temple of Tinia.

10 G. Sassatelli and E. Govi, *Marzabotto: la casa 1 della regio 4, insula 2*, p. 30.

11 This is the central thesis put forward by Sassatelli and Govi. Their concluding remarks are apt in the context of this discussion: 'the temple . . . represented a social *and* religious meeting point for all the *citizens*.' Ibid., p. 36; emphasis mine.

12 Ibid., p. 27.

13 G. Sassatelli and E. Govi, *Culti, forma urbana e artigianato a Marzabotto. Nuove prospettive di ricerca: Atti del Convegno di Studi Bologna, S. Giovanni in Monte 3–4 giugno 2003* (Bologna, 2005), pp. 47–55.

14 Plato, *The Republic*, 433a–433b.

15 Aristotle, *Politics*, 2: 1267b.

16 For more on Hippodamus as a planner, see A. Burns, 'Hippodamus and the Planned City', *Historia: Zeitschrift für Alte Geschichte*, 4 (1976), pp. 414–28. D. W. Gill, 'Hippodamus and the Piraeus', *Historia: Zeitschrift für Alte Geschichte*, 55 (2006), pp. 1–15, explores his work at the Piraeus, while J. C. Hogan, 'Hippodamus on the Best Form of Government

and Law', *Political Research Quarterly*, 12 (1956), pp. 763–83, presents Hippodamus as political philosopher. R. Paden, 'The Two Professions of Hippodamus of Miletus', *Philosophy & Geography*, IV (2001), pp. 25–48, argues persuasively that it is only by understanding Hippodamus as both planner *and* philosopher that we can appreciate his career.

17 Aristotle, *Politics*, 2: 1267b:22–8.

18 C. Nicolet, *The World of the Citizen in Republican Rome* (Berkeley, CA, 1980), pp. 21–3, draws out this particular incident from Livy's *History of Rome*, book 1.13.4.

19 The major publication on Roman magistrates is the magisterial work of T. S. Broughton, *The Magistrates of the Roman Republic* (Oxford, 1951) (pun intended).

20 Cicero uses the concept of *civitas* in numerous cases, but defines it clearly in *Somnium Scipionis*, C3.

21 For Acquarossa, see C. E. Östenburg and M. Pallottino, *Case etrusche di Acquarossa* (Rome, 1975).

22 See C. Ambus and I. Krauskopf, 'The Curved Staff in the Ancient Near East as a Predecessor of the Etruscan Lituus', in *Etrusco Ritu: Material Aspects of Etruscan Religion*, ed. L. B. van der Meer (Leuven, 2010), pp. 127–53.

23 A. Maggiani, 'Appunti sulle magistrature etrusche', *Studi Etruschi*, 62 (1996), pp. 95–138, reviews the evidence for magistrates in Etruria. For the Rubiera inscription, see C. De Simone, *Le iscrizioni etrusche dei cippi di Rubiera* (Reggio Emilia, 1992).

24 This weight is rather late in date (third century BCE), but it remains interesting. See Maggiani, ibid., p. 101.

25 M. Morandi Tarabella, *Prosopographia etrusca*, vol. I (Rome, 2004), pp. 167–8.

26 According to Dionysius of Halicarnassus (*Roman Antiquities*, 1:30), that is. See H. Rix, 'Etr. Mes rasnal = lat. Res publica', in *Studi di antichita in onore di G. Maetzke II*, ed. G. Maetzke, M.G.M. Costagli and L. T. Perna (Rome, 1984), pp. 455–68, for a longer discussion of the word *Rasna* and its use in context in Etruscan texts.

27 See P. Ducati's works, *Storia dell'arte etrusca* (Florence, 1927) and *Etruria antica* (Bologna, 1927) for his very obvious fascist views.

28 The incident is described in context with other Nazi war crimes in Italy by P. Cooke, 'Recent Work on Nazi Massacres in Italy During the Second World War', *Modern Italy*, V (2000), pp. 211–18. See also E. Spagnoletti, *The Massacres in Marzabotto and Bologna during World War II and their Contemporary Ramifications* (Rome, 1980) for a more detailed analysis, in addition to a discussion of the growing tensions in and around Bologna.

29 You can still see some of the damaged artefacts in the museum today.

8 Sex, Lies and Etruscans

1 S. Haynes, *Etruscan Civilization: A Cultural History* (Oxford, 2005), p. 147. The shock value of female nudity, even for the goddess Aphrodite,

is visible in the reception of the Aphrodite of Cnidos, acknowledged as the first naked female statue displayed in Greece.

2 There is some argument over the source of the marble for the main figure: L. Bonfante, 'Nudity as a Costume in Classical Art', *American Journal of Archaeology*, XCIII (1989), pp. 543–70, esp. p. 566, suggests that it came from Paros, while the original consensus of A. Andren, 'Il santuario della Necropoli di Cannicella ad Orvieto', *Studi Etruschi*, XXXV (1967), pp. 41–85, esp. p. 50, was that the marble was sourced from Naxos.

3 M. Cristofani, 'La "Venere" della Cannicella', *Santuario e culto nella necropoli di Cannicella. Annali della Fondazione per il Museo Claudio Faina*, 3 (1987), pp. 30–31.

4 This analysis is that of G. Colonna, 'I culti del santuario della Cannicella', in *Santuario e culto nella necropoli di Cannicella. Relazione e interventi nel convegno del 1984*, ed. G. Pugliese Carratelli (Florence, 1987), pp. 11–26.

5 A. Andren, 'Il santuario della Necropoli di Cannicella', p. 45.

6 For which see R. Benassai, 'Per una lettura del programma figurativo delle Tomba delle Bighe di Tarquinia', *Orizzonti. Rassegna di archeologia*, 2 (2001), pp. 51–62; B. D'Agostino and L. Cerchiai, *Il mare, la morte, l'amore: gli Etruschi, i Greci e l'immagine* (Rome, 1999), p. 68, remark on the intriguing contrast between images of couples and images of homosexual encounters within the same tombs.

7 Theopompus of Chios, *Histories*, 115.

8 M. A. Flower, *Theopompus of Chios: History and Rhetoric in the Fourth Century BC* (Oxford, 1997) provides a rich biography of Theopompus, including his time in Athens.

9 T. Harrison, *Greeks and Barbarians* (London, 2002) provides an excellent discussion of Greek/barbarian encounters and recounts this stereotype.

10 E. Hall, 'Asia Unmanned: Images of Victory in Classical Athens', in *War and Society in the Greek World*, ed. J. Rich and G. Shipley (London, 1993), pp. 108–33, provides a detailed analysis of the Greek sources that systematically feminize the Persian foe.

11 Athenaeus of Naucratis, *Deipnosophistae*, book 12, 529a.

12 Flower, *Theopompus of Chios*, p. 95, makes a convincing argument connecting Theopompus' sexual slurs with those critical of both Aristippus and the Athenian statesman Alcibiades.

13 C. Dix, *D. H. Lawrence and Women* (London, 1980) considers at length Lawrence's relationships with different women, including these major players in his life.

14 D. H. Lawrence, *Sketches of Etruscan Places* (London, 1932), p. 127.

15 Ibid., p. 138.

16 V. Bellelli, 'Vei: nome, competenze e particolarità di una divinità etrusca', in *Antropologia e archeologia in confronto: rappresentazioni e pratiche del sacro*, ed. V. Nizzo and L. LaRocca (Rome, 2012), pp. 455–78.

9 Wrapped Up Writings

1 For more on these remarkable letters see M. M. Terras, *Image to Interpretation: An Intelligent System to Aid Historians in Reading the Vindolanda Texts* (Oxford, 2006).
2 If you want to read Etruscan, purchase G. Bonfante and L. Bonfante, *The Etruscan Language* (Manchester, 2001). R. Wallace, *Zikh Rasna: A Manual of the Etruscan Language and Inscriptions* (Ann Arbor, MI, 2008) also provides an excellent manual, but is a little harder to find outside the USA.
3 This example is catalogued as Vatican Museo Gregorio Etrusco 14949.
4 For the extraordinary adventures of the Zagreb mummy, see I. Uranić, 'Contributions to the Provenance of the Zagreb Mummy', *Acta Antiqua*, 46 (2006), pp. 197–202; A. Rendić-Miočević, *Notes on the Accession of the Zagreb Mummy and her Wrapping* (Zagreb, 1997); and M. Flury-Lemberg, 'Rekonstrukcija Zagrebačke lanene knjige ili povoja Zagrebačke mumije', *Vjesnik Arheološkog muzeja u Zagrebu*, 19 (1987), pp. 73–92. It is also recounted in prefaces to the texts themselves, for which see L. B. van der Meer, *Liber linteus zagrabiensis* (Leuven, 2007).
5 I. Mirnik and A. Rendić-Miočević, 'Liber Linteus Zagrabiensis ii', *Vjesnik Arheoloskog muzeja u Zagrebu*, XX (1987), pp. 31–48. Mirnik and Rendić-Miočević present a series of correspondence regarding this phase in the mummy's history: in the Italian text that accompanies the letters is a summary of the relationship between Brugsch and Burton (1987: 42).
6 This exemplar table is loosely adapted from C. D. Buck, *A Dictionary of Selected Synonyms in the Principal Indo-European languages* (Chicago, IL, 2008 [1947]). There are extensive examples for each word in Buck's dictionary, ibid., pp. 2.36, 3.41, 1.31.
7 This problematic term is developed by H. Rix, *Rätisch und Etruskisch* (Innsbruck, 1998).
8 This idea reached its nadir in the work of J. G. Stickel, *Das Etruskische durch Erklärung von Inschriften und Namen als semit. Sprache erwiesen* (Leipzig, 1858).
9 This argument is strongly associated with the work of F. C. Woudhuizen, *Etruscan as a Colonial Luwian Language* (Innsbruck, 2008).
10 This discredited idea was put forward in Z. Mayani, *The Etruscans Begin to Speak* (London, 1962). G. Bonfante and L. Bonfante, in *The Etruscan Language* (Manchester, 2002), p. xii, even mention that relationships have been posited between Etruscan and Aztec.
11 This example comes from ibid., p. 137. For 'za' see also J. Hadas-Lebel, 'L'œnochoé putlumza: un pocolom étrusque?', *Collection de la Maison de l'Orient méditerranéen ancien. Série philologique*, 43 (2009), pp. 273–85.
12 This example is from G. Bonfante and L. Bonfante, *The Etruscan Language*, p. 101, TLE 43.
13 This is his *Volumen libris septuaginta distinctum de antiquitatibus et gestis Etruscorum*. See G. Bonucci Caporali, ed., *Annio da Viterbo: Documenti e ricerche* (Rome, 1981).

14 This ruthless unmasking of Annio da Viterbo was the work of Girolamo Mei, in a short Latin treatise 'On the Origins of the City of Florence' (1565).
15 The discovery is chronicled by M. Pallottino, *Scavi nel santuario Etrusco di Pyrgi: relazione preliminare della settima campagna, 1964, e scoperta di tre lamine d'oro inscritte in Etrusco e in Punico* (Rome, 1964), and contextualized further by G. Colonna, 'Il santuario di Pyrgi alla luce delle recenti scoperte', *Studi Etruschi*, XXXIII (1965), pp. 193–219.
16 For the translation of the Phoenician text from Pyrgi, see P. C. Schmitz, 'The Phoenician Text from the Etruscan Sanctuary at Pyrgi', *Journal of the American Oriental Society*, CXV (1995), pp. 559–75. He also provides an extended bibliography for the plaques themselves.
17 This phrase is adapted from G. Bonfante and L. Bonfante, *The Etruscan Language*, p. 12.
18 O. Wikander, 'The Religio-social Message of the Gold Tablets from Pyrgi', *Opuscula*, 1 (2008), pp. 78–84, emphasizes the political role of the texts, and their connecting of earthly power with divine favour.
19 The dating of the Zagreb text is still problematic: the linen itself may have been woven as early as the fourth century BCE, but the writing is almost certainly later. R.Wallace, 'Review: Il Liber Linteus di Zagabria. Testualità e Contenuto (Biblioteca di "Studi Etruschi" 50) by Valentina Belfiore', *Etruscan Studies*, XV (2012), pp. 232–7, suggests the late third or early second century, while J. M. Turfa, *Divining the Etruscan World: The Brontoscopic Calendar and Religious Practice* (Cambridge, 2012), p. 24, is fixed on the latter part of this range. It was recycled into its present bandage format even later, in the first century BCE.
20 Dionysius of Halicarnassus (*Roman Antiquities*, 7:5–6) describes the battle in detail, but see A. B. Gallia, 'Reassessing the "Cumaean Chronicle": Greek Chronology and Roman History in Dionysius of Halicarnassus', *Journal of Roman Studies*, XCVII (2007), pp. 50–67, for a critical assessment of his account.
21 See J. Kaimio, *The Ousting of Etruscan by Latin in Etruria* (Helsinki, 1972), for more on the linguistic conquest of Etruscan by Latin, and L. Ceccarelli, 'The Romanization of Etruria', in *A Companion to the Etruscans*, ed. S. Bell and A. Carpino (New York, 2015), pp. 28–40, for an up-to-date account of Roman power in Etruria.
22 The fascinating and largely forgotten figure of Plautia Urgulanilla appears in Sutonius' study of Claudius within the *Lives of the Caesars* at regular intervals (throughout books 5 and 6).
23 D. Briquel, 'Que savons-nous des "Tyrrhenika" de l'empereur Claude?', *Rivista di filologia e di istruzione classica*, 116 (1988), pp. 448–70, provides a thorough analysis of Claudius' passion for all things Etruscan.
24 A summary derived from van der Meer, *Liber linteus zagrabiensis*.
25 A. Bouchard-Cote et al., 'Automated Reconstruction of Ancient Languages Using Probabilistic Models of Sound Change', *Proceedings of the National Academy of Sciences*, 110 (2013), pp. 4224–9.

26 L. Agostiniani and F. Nicosia, *Tabula cortonensi* (Rome, 2000), and A. Bottini, 'Gentlemen of Cortona', *Etruscan Studies*, VII (2000), pp. 3–4.

10 Listening to Livers

1 L. B. van der Meer, *The Bronze Liver of Placenza* (Leiden, 1987) provides a full analysis of the Piacenza Liver – its original production somewhere near Chiusi, its discovery and its ritual context. See also A. Morandi, 'Nuove osservazioni sul fegato bronzeo di Piacenza', *Mélanges de l'Ecole française de Rome Antiquité*, C (1988), pp. 283–97.

2 F. Arisi, *Il Museo Civico di Piacenza* (Piacenza, 1960), pp. 199–203, describes the discovery in detail, as does L. B. van der Meer, *The Bronze Liver of Piacenza: Analysis of a Polytheistic Structure* (Amsterdam, 1987), p. 5.

3 These were described by M. Jastrow, 'Hepatoscopy and Astrology in Babylonia and Assyria', *Proceedings of the American Philosophical Society*, 47 (1908), pp. 646–76, but have formed part of wider studies of Babylonian ritual by A. Reiner, 'Astral Magic in Babylonia', *Transactions of the American Philosophical Society*, 85 (1995), pp. 1–150, and D. Pardee, 'Divinatory and Sacrificial Rites', *Near Eastern Archaeology*, LXIII (2000), pp. 232–4.

4 See U. Koch, *Babylonian Liver Omens: The Chapters Manzāzu, Padānu and Pān Tākalti of the Babylonian Extispicy Series Mainly from Aššurbanipal's Library* (Copenhagen, 2000); U. Koch, 'Sheep and Sky: Systems of Divinatory Interpretation', in *The Oxford Handbook of Cuneiform Culture*, ed. K. Radner and E. Robson (Oxford, 2011), pp. 447–69.

5 See U. S. Koch, *Mesopotamian Astrology: An Introduction to Babylonian and Assyrian Celestial Divination* (Cambridge, 1995); and G. Beckman, 'Mesopotamians and Mesopotamian Learning at Hattuša', *Journal of Cuneiform Studies*, XXXV (1983), pp. 97–111 for Hittite liver models.

6 See, for example, L. Stieda, 'Anatomisches Über alt-italische Weihgeschenke (Donaria)', *Anatomy and Embryology*, XVI (1901), pp. 1–82. A more nuanced and subtle form of this argument is made by D. Collins, 'Mapping the Entrails: The Practice of Greek Hepatoscopy', *American Journal of Philology*, CXXIX (2008), pp. 319–46.

7 M. Pallottino, *The Etruscans* (London, 1975), p. 154, provides a summation of the *Libri Tagetici* and its context and place in the tiny surviving canon of Etruscan religious literature.

8 Cicero, *On Divination*, 2.50; Ovid, *Metamorphoses*, 15:552.

9 J. R. Wood, 'The Myth of Tages', *Latomus*, 39 (1980), pp. 325–44, brings together the evidence for the myth, and argues for its authenticity as an Etruscan tale, not a Roman appendix.

10 This mirror is first described by M. Pallottino, *Uno specchio di Tuscania e la leggenda etrusca di Tarchon* (Rome, 1930), p. 49, but see also M. Torelli, '"Etruria principes disciplinam doceto" il mito normativo dello specchio di Tuscania', *Studia Tarquiniensia (Archaeologia Perusina)*, IX (1988), pp. 109–18.

11 M. Bonghi Jovino, *Gli Etruschi di Tarquinia* (Modena, 1986), p. 392; G. Colonna, 'Una proposta per il supposto elogio tarquiniese di Tarchon', in *Tarquinia: scavi ricerche e prospettive*, ed. M. Bonghi Jovino and C. Chiaramente Trere (Milan, 1987), pp. 153–7.

12 J. Heurgon, 'The Date of Vegoia's Prophecy', *Journal of Roman Studies*, XLIX (1959), pp. 41–5, argued that Vegoia/Vecu should really be considered a kind of nymph rather than a prophetess. See also A. Valvo, *La 'Profezia di Vegoia': proprietà fondiaria e aruspicina in Etruria nel I secolo A.C.* (Rome, 1991) for an expanded consideration of the significance of Vegoia/Vecu, and the social context of her revelations.

13 For a recent assessment of cuniculi, see C. Bizzari and D. Soren, 'Etruscan Domestic Architecture, Hydraulic Engineering, and Water Management Technologies', in *A Companion to the Etruscans*, ed. S. Bell and A. A. Carpino (Hoboken, NJ, 2016), pp. 129–45.

14 This term is defined in O.A.W. Dilke, *Mathematics and Measurement* (Berkeley, CA, 1988), p. 293. K. M. Phillips, 'Bryn Mawr College Excavations in Tuscany 1971', *American Journal of Archaeology*, LXXVI (1972), pp. 249–55, on p. 251, describes the frieze plaques from the Archaic period building at Poggio Civitate (Murlo) as measuring two Italic feet, hence this date. A shipwreck dating to the fifth century BCE preserved a wooden builder's square that seemingly correlates to this measurement of 27 cm (R. R. Stieglitz, 'Classical Greek Measures and the Builder's Instruments from the Ma'agan Mikhael Shipwreck', *American Journal of Archaeology*, CX (2006), pp. 195–203, esp. p. 200).

15 Pliny the Elder, *Natural History*, 2:137–9.

16 S. Hammond, *Iconography of the Etruscan Haruspex* (Edinburgh, 2009) presents a catalogue of images of divination in Etruria.

17 For the figure of the priestess or hatrencu (female haruspex) in Etruria see L. E. Lundeen, 'In Search of the Etruscan Priestess: A Re-examination of the Hatrencu', in *Religion in Republican Italy*, ed. C. E. Shultz and P. B. Harvey (Cambridge, 2006), pp. 34–61.

18 Temple architecture in Etruria is a complex issue, grossly simplified here. For a more complex and thought-provoking discussion see V. Izzet, 'Tuscan Order: The Development of Etruscan Sanctuary Architecture', in *Religion in Archaic and Republican Rome and Italy: Evidence and Experience*, ed. C. Smith and E. Bispham (Edinburgh, 2000), pp. 34–53, and V. Izzet, 'Form and Meaning in Etruscan Ritual Space', *Cambridge Archaeological Journal*, XI (2001), pp. 185–200, as a starting point, and C. R. Potts, *Religious Architecture in Latium and Etruria, c. 900–500 BC* (Oxford, 2015) for a detailed, in-depth study.

19 A lovely consideration of this phenomenon is R. Bradley, *The Passage of Arms* (Cambridge, 1990).

20 P. G. Warden et al., 'Poggio Colla: An Etruscan Settlement of the 7th–2nd c. BC (1998–2004 excavations)', *Journal of Roman Archaeology*, XVIII (2005), pp. 252–66; P. G. Warden and M. L. Thomas, 'Sanctuary and

Settlement: Archaeological Work at Poggio Colla (Vicchio di Mugello)', *Etruscan Studies*, IX (2002), pp. 97–108.

21 This deposit is described in P. G. Warden, 'Remains of the Ritual at the Sanctuary of Poggio Colla', in *Votives, Places, and Rituals in Etruscan Religion: Studies in Honour of Jean MacIntosh Turfa*, ed. M. Gleba and H. Becker (Leiden, 2009), pp. 107–22, esp. pp. 111–13.

22 M. Gleba, 'Textile Tools in Ancient Italian Votive Contexts: Evidence of Dedication or Production?', in *Votives, Places and Rituals in Etruscan Religion: Studies in Honour of Jean MacIntosh Turfa*, ed. M. Gleba and H. S. Becker (Leiden, 2009), pp. 69–84. D. Gill, 'METRU.MENECE: An Etruscan Painted Inscription on a Mid-5th-century BC Red-figure Cup from Populonia', *Antiquity*, LXI (1987), pp. 82–7. A wide range of different objects carry such inscriptions: Gleba considers the dedication of textile tools, while Gill provides a contextualization of dedicatory inscriptions on pottery in Etruria.

23 For anatomical votives in Etruria, see J. M. Turfa, 'Anatomical Votives and Italian Medical Traditions', in *Murlo and the Etruscans: Art and Society in Ancient Etruria*, ed. R. de Puma and J. P. Small (Madison, WI, 1994), pp. 224–40; J. M. Turfa, 'Anatomical Votives', *ThesCRA I* (2004), pp. 359–68.

24 S. Stopponi, 'Orvieto, Campo della Fiera – Fanum Voltumnae', in *The Etruscan World*, ed. J. M. Turfa (London, 2015), pp. 632–54, esp. p. 632, outlines the blurring of a local god, Voltumna, to Tinia.

25 For Pyrgi see Turfa, ed., *The Etruscan World*: M. P. Baglione, 'The Sanctuary of Pyrgi', ibid., pp. 613–31, esp. p. 617, and for the Ara della Regina see G. Bagnasco Gianni, 'Tarquinia: Excavations by the University of Milan at the Ara della Regina Sanctuary' and 'Tarquinia. Sacred Spaces and Sanctuaries', pp. 594–612, esp. p. 559.

26 I. Edlund-Berry, 'Gods and Places in Etruscan Religion', *Etruscan Studies*, I (1994), pp. 11–22, emphasizes the unsurprisingly close connection between deities and their specific places of worship within the landcape.

27 For a full discussion of the Etruscan deities, see E. Simon, 'Gods in Harmony: The Etruscan Pantheon', in *The Religion of the Etruscans*, ed. N. T. de Grummond and E. Simon (Austin, TX, 2006), pp. 45–65, for a broad introduction to the Etruscan pantheon, their relationships to Greek and Roman deities and with each other.

28 S. Kennedy Quigley, 'Visual Representations of the Birth of Athena/Minerva: A Comparative Study', *Etruscan Studies*, VIII (2001), pp. 65–78, develops an in-depth analysis of the representation of Athena/Menrva in Etruria, focusing on her birth from Tinia. See also G. Colonna, 'Minerva', in *Lexicon iconographicorum mythologiae Classicae Volume II* (Zurich, 1984), pp. 1050–74, for a full consideration of Etruscan Menrva.

29 J. R. Jannot, *Religion in Ancient Etruria* (Madison, WI, 2005), p. 156, makes this point.

30 *Epic of Gilgamesh*, tablet VI.

31 See P. Albenda, 'The "Queen of the Night" Plaque: A Revisit', *Journal of the American Oriental Society*, CXXV (2005), pp. 171–90; and D. Collon, 'The Queen under Attack – A Rejoinder', *Iraq*, 69 (2007), pp. 45–51. For more on the representation of Ishtar and her relationship to women's lives in ancient Mesopotamia, see Z. Bahrani, *Women of Babylon: Gender and Representation in Mesopotamia* (London, 2001).

32 For her transition from the Near East to the Mediterranean, see A. E. Barclay, 'The Potnia Theron: Adaptation of a Near Eastern Image', in *Potnia: Deities and Religion in the Aegean Bronze Age*, ed. R. Laffineur and R. Hägg (Liege, 2001), pp. 373–81. For Potnia Theron in Etruria, see H. Damgaard Andersen, 'The Origin of Potnia Theron in Central Italy', *Hamburger Beiträge zur Archäologie*, XIX (1992), pp. 73–113.

33 A. S. Tuck, personal correspondence with the author.

34 This is the central hypothesis of J. M. Turfa, 'Etruscan Religion at the Watershed: Before and After the Fourth Century BCE', in *Religion in Republican Italy*, ed. C. E. Shultz and P. B. Harvey (Cambridge, 2006), pp. 62–85.

35 Suetonius describes Spurinna's role in the assassination of Caesar (*Lives of the Caesars*, 81–9), as do Plutarch (*Lives*, 63–6) and Cicero (*On Divination*, 1.1119). J. T. Ramsey, '"Beware the Ides of March!": An Astrological Prediction?', *Classical Quarterly (New Series)*, 50 (2000), pp. 440–54, offers a critical assessment of the events of the Ides of March, including Spurinna's part.

36 E. Orlin, *Foreign Cults in Rome: Creating the Roman Empire* (Oxford, 2010), p. 92, argues that the haruspices deliberately and carefully integrated their rituals into the Etruscan state. J. Rupke, 'Divination romaine et rationalité grecque dans la Rome du IIe siècle avant notre ère', in *La raison des signes: Présages, rites, destin dans les sociétés de la méditerranée ancienne*, ed. S. Georgoudi and R. Koch Piettre (Paris, 2011), pp. 479–500 (p. 337), lists the individuals who kept personal Etruscan soothsayers in their train, which includes the great general Sulla.

37 This is the argument made convincingly by D. Briquel, 'Tages Against Jesus: Etruscan Religion in the Late Roman Empire', *Etruscan Studies*, X (2007), pp. 153–61.

38 Tertullian, *Apology*, 35.12.

39 The court haruspices found that they could no longer predict the future, and blamed the Christians for the failure of their rituals. Diocletian then sent the imperial haruspex to the oracle of Apollo at Didyma: surprise, surprise, the oracle confirmed that the Christians must be purged. See J. Fontenrose, *Didyma: Apollo's Oracle, Cult, and Companions* (Berkeley, CA, 1988), p. 24, and the primary source, Lactantius, *De Mortibus persecutorum*, 10.1–5.

40 This is the hypothesis of L. Bonfante, 'Iconografia delle madri: Etruria e Italia antica', in *Le donne in Etruria*, ed. A. Rallo (Rome, 1989), pp. 85–106.

11 Facing Oblivion

1 See M. Cristofani, *Etruschi: una nuova immagine* (Rome, 2000), p. 20, and U. Calzoni, 'Recenti scoperte a "Grotta Lattaia" sulla Montagna di Cetona', *Studi Etruschi*, IX (1940), pp. 301–4.

2 G. Paolucci and A. Minetti, eds, *Sarteano etrusca: Collezionismo, antiquariato e scoperte archeologiche ottocentesche* (Montepulciano, 1989), and A. Minetti and A. Rastrelli, *La necropoli della Palazzina nel Museo civico archeologico di Sarteano* (Montepulciano, 2001) describe the history of excavations.

3 A. Minetti, 'La tomba della Quadriga infernale di Sarteano', *Studi Etruschi*, LXX (2004), pp. 135–59, and A. Minetti, 'Sarteano (SI): necropoli delle Pianacce: campagna di scavo 2005', *Notiziario della Soprintendenza per i Beni Archeologici della Toscana*, I (2005), pp. 425–8, reports the discovery, while her later works (A. Minetti, *La tomba della quadriga infernale nella necropoli delle Pianacce di Sarteano* (Rome, 2006); 'La tomba dipinta di Sarteano', *Ostraka*, XVI (2008), pp. 79–91) describe the paintings in detail.

4 A. Minetti, 'Sculture funerarie in pietra fetida dalla necropoli delle Pianacce di Sarteano', *Studi Etruschi*, LXXIV (2008), pp. 125–39, focuses on the sculpture from the Pianacce necropolis.

5 Minetti describes the process of conserving and preparing the tomb for the public to visit in her 2006 volume, cited above, A. Minetti, *La tomb a della quadriga infernale nella necropoli delle Pianacce di Sarteano* (Rome, 2006).

6 A. Maccari, 'Un funerale chiusino: appunti su un cippo inedito di Sarteano', *Rivista di archeologia*, XXXV (2011), pp. 5–15, considers the process of an Etruscan funeral at Sarteano in detail.

7 L. J. Taylor, 'Performing the Prothesis: Gender, Gesture, Ritual and Role on the Chiusine Reliefs from Archaic Etruria', *Etruscan Studies*, XVII (2014), pp. 1–27, interrogates the Etruscan prothesis ritual at length.

8 P. J. Holliday, 'Processional Imagery in Late Etruscan Funerary Art', *American Journal of Archaeology*, XCIV (1990), pp. 73–93, considers the significance of processions in Etruscan burials and funerals.

9 L. Pieraccini, 'Families, Feasting, and Funerals: Funerary Ritual at Ancient Caere', *Etruscan Studies*, VII (2000), pp. 35–50, argues for the centrality of feasting to Etruscan funerary ritual.

10 This is the view put forward by G. Moscatelli, 'Gli enigmatici affreschi della tomba della quadriga infernale di Sarteano: amicizia o amore?', *Archeotuscia News*, 1 (2012), pp. 10–11.

11 J. Elliot, 'The Etruscan Wolfman in Myth and Ritual', *Etruscan Studies*, II (1994), pp. 17–34, describes the wolf-like countenance of one particular Etruscan demon, while F. Roncalli, 'Laris Pulenas and Sisyphus: Mortals, Heroes and Demons in the Etruscan Underworld', *Etruscan Studies*, CXI (1996), pp. 45–64, explores other demonic figures.

12 This is the Tomb of the Reliefs, for which see H. Blanck and G. Proietti, *La tomba dei Rilievi di Cerveteri* (Rome, 1986).

13 K. Hostetler, 'Serpent Iconography', *Etruscan Studies*, x (2004), pp. 203–10, develops this idea.
14 See A. S. Tuck, 'On the Origin of Vanth: Death Harbingers and Banshees in Etruscan and Celtic Worlds', in *New Perspectives on Etruria and Rome: Papers in Honour of Richard Daniel De Puma*, ed. S. Bell and H. Nagy (Madison, WI, 2009), pp. 251–63, for more on the identity and origins of Vanth.
15 This is particularly visible in the Tuscania survey evidence, for which see G. Barker and T. Rasmussen, 'The Archaeology of an Etruscan Polis: A Preliminary Report on the Tuscania Project (1986 and 1987 seasons)', *Papers of the British School at Rome*, 56 (1988), pp. 25–42.
16 For the toga see L. Bonfante, *Etruscan Dress* (Baltimore, MD, 1975) and H. Granger-Taylor, 'Weaving Clothes to Shape in the Ancient World: The Tunic and Toga of the Arringatore', *Textile History*, XIII (1982), pp. 3–25.
17 As described in the previous chapter, see Tertullian, *Apology*, 35.12.
18 This argument is that of R. H. Rough, 'Enrico Scrovegni, the Cavalieri Gaudenti, and the Arena Chapel in Padua', *Art Bulletin*, 62 (1980), pp. 24–35, in his examination of the commissioner of the chapel, Enrico Scrovegni.
19 This interview is contained within D. T. Van Velzen, 'The World of Tuscan Tomb Robbers: Living with the Local Community and the Ancestors', *International Journal of Cultural Property*, V (1996), pp. 111–26, which also contains a history of the *tombaroli* phenomenon.
20 This research is presented within V. S. Manzon and E. Gualdi Rosso, 'Health Patterns of the Etruscan Population (6th–3rd Centuries BC) in Northern Italy: The Case of Spina', *International Journal of Osteoarchaeology*, X (2015), pp. 24–38.
21 For this remarkable woman, see the papers collected in J. Swaddling and J. Prag, eds, *Seianti Hanunia Tlesnasa: The Story of an Etruscan Noblewoman* British Museum Occasional Paper 100 (London, 2002).
22 Reported in *Il Tirrenico* newspaper on 22 October 2015.

FURTHER READING

If you would like to read more about the Etruscans (and I hope you do, as this book only skims the surface), there are three titles in particular that I recommend. These are:

Izzet, V., *The Archaeology of Etruscan Society* (Cambridge, 2007)
Smith, C., *The Etruscans: A Very Short Introduction* (Oxford, 2013)
If you are feeling extravagant, then the most comprehensive (and expensive) of the three may be for you:
Turfa, J. M., ed., *The Etruscan World* (London, 2015)

Classical Sources

Aristotle, *Politics*, trans. C.D.C. Reeve (Cambridge, 1997)
Boccaccio, *De mulieribus claris*, trans. V. Brown (Boston, MA, 2001)
Cassius Dio, *Roman History*, trans. I. Scott-Kilvert (London, 1987)
Cicero, *On Divination*, trans. D. Wardle (Oxford, 2006)
Cicero, *The Dream of Scipio*, trans. P. Bullock (New York, 1983)
Diogenes Laertius, *Lives of the Eminent Philosophers*, trans R. D. Hicks (Boston, MA, 2000)
Dionysius of Halicarnassus, *Roman Antiquities*, trans. E. Cary (London, 1968)
Herodotus, *The Histories*, trans. R. Waterfield (Oxford, 2008)
'Hymn to Dionysus', in *Homeric Hymns*, trans. S. Ruden (Cambridge, 2005), pp. 1–3, 67–8
Lactantius, *De Mortibus persecutorum*, trans. J. L. Creed (Oxford, 1985)
Livy, *History of Rome*, trans. R. M. Ogilvie and A. de Selincourt (London, 2002)
Ovid, *Metamorphoses*, trans. C. Martin (London, 2005)
Plato, *The Republic*, trans G.M.A. Grube (Cambridge, 1992)
Plutarch, *Lives*, trans. B. Perrin (London, 1994)
Suetonius, *Lives of the Caesars*, trans. C. Edwards (Cambridge, 2008)
Tacitus, *Agricola*, trans. H. Mattingly (London, 2010)

Tacitus, *The Annals of Imperial Rome*, trans. M. Grant (London, 1973)
Tertullian, *Apology*, trans R. D. Sider (Washington, DC, 2000)
Theopompus of Chios, *Histories*, in Athenaeus, *Deipnosophistae*, trans. C. Burton Gulick (London, 1927)
Thucydides, *Histories vol I and vol II*, trans. H. Stuart-Jones (Oxford, 1963)

ACKNOWLEDGEMENTS

Thank you so much to all the wonderful people I have met working in Etruscan archaeology: from museum attendants to professors, it has been an absolute privilege.

Vedia Izzet was the first person to introduce me to the Etruscans, while Tony Tuck taught me how to bring them to life during my time digging at Poggio Civitate. Theresa Huntsman, Eoin O'Donoghue, Kate Kreindler and Fredrik Tobin have been stalwart colleagues as well as good friends, while Andrew Carroll and Jan Freedman offered themselves as readers of early drafts with great generosity. Theresa Huntsman also kindly provided some of her photographs to use in this book.

The draft of the text of this book was completed during a Visiting Fellowship at the Moore Institute, National University of Ireland, Galway. I am deeply grateful to Edward Herring and Daniel Carey for their support during my time there.

I am also grateful to the Soprintendenza per I Beni Culturali for permission to use some of their images, and to the team at ArtRes New York for their assistance in securing others.

My editors at Reaktion, Ben and Amy, deserve great thanks for their patience and skill. Yvonne Marshall, Denise Allen and Oliver Gilkes taught me how to write (for very different audiences). My parents taught me how to think: an even more precious gift.

The majority of this book was written during the first year of my daughter's life – it would have been an impossible task if not for my husband's untiring support, and her ability to nap and feed to the soundtrack of typing. Phil and Silvia, this is for both of you.

PHOTO ACKNOWLEDGEMENTS

© Sebastian Ballard: p. 25; © Trustees of the British Museum: p. 50; © HIP, Art Resource, NY: p. 100; Digital images courtesy of the Getty's Open Content Program: pp. 68, 74, 75; Theresa Huntsman and Soprintendenza per i Beni Culturali Toscana: pp. 170, 171; © Erich Lessing Art Resource, NY: p. 19; © Metropolitan Museum of Art, NY (Open Access Programme): pp. 33, 35, 36, 40, 48, 51, 54, 55, 59, 70, 72, 73, 76, 77 , 81, 85, 86, 87, 92, 94, 97, 101, 119, 120, 127, 133, 136, 138, 142, 148, 150, 157, 161, 166, 168, 173; © Nimatallah, Art Resource, NY: p. 84; © Gianni Dagli Orti The Art Archive at Art Resource, NY: pp. 111, 122; © Alfredo Dagli Orti, The Art Archive at Art Resource, NY: p. 147; © Scala, Art Resource, NY: p. 153; Scala, Ministero per i Beni e le Attività culturali, Art Resource, NY: p. 30; © Soprintendenza per i beni culturali archeologici Toscana: p. 62.

INDEX